Library of
Davidson College

Decision-Making in Communist Countries: An Inside View

Jan Sejna
Joseph D. Douglass, Jr.

Foreign Policy Report
January 1986

A Publication of the
INSTITUTE FOR FOREIGN POLICY ANALYSIS, INC.
Cambridge, Massachusetts, and Washington, D.C.

PERGAMON·BRASSEY'S
International Defense Publishers

Washington New York Oxford Toronto Sydney Frankfurt

Pergamon Press Offices:

U.S.A.	Pergamon-Brassey's International Defense Publishers, 1340 Old Chain Bridge Road, McLean, Virginia, 22101, U.S.A.
	Pergamon Press Inc., Maxwell House, Fairview Park, Elmsford, New York 10523, U.S.A.
U.K.	Pergamon Press Ltd., Headington Hill Hall, Oxford OX3 0BW, England
CANADA	Pergamon Press Canada Ltd., Suite 104, 150 Consumers Road, Willowdale, Ontario M2J 1P9, Canada
AUSTRALIA	Pergamon Press (Aust.) Pty. Ltd., P.O. Box 544, Potts Point, NSW 2011, Australia
FEDERAL REPUBLIC OF GERMANY	Pergamon Press GmbH, Hammerweg 6, D-6242 Kronberg-Taunus, Federal Republic of Germany
BRAZIL	Pergamon Editora Ltda., Rua Eça de Queiros, 346, CEP 04011, São Paulo, Brazil
JAPAN	Pergamon Press Ltd., 8th Floor, Matsuoka Central Building, 1-7-1 Nishishinjuku, Shinjuku, Tokyo 160, Japan
PEOPLE'S REPUBLIC OF CHINA	Pergamon Press, Qianmen Hotel, Beijing, People's Republic of China

Copyright © 1986 Institute for Foreign Policy Analysis, Inc.

All rights reserved. No part of this publication may be reproduced, stored in a retrieval system or transmitted in any form or by any means: electronic, electrostatic, magnetic tape, mechanical, photocopying, recording or otherwise, without permission in writing from the publishers.

First printing 1986

Library of Congress Cataloging in Publication Data

Sejna, Jan, 1927-
    Decision-making in communist countries.

    (Foreign policy report)
    "A publication of the Institute for Foreign Policy Analysis, Inc."
    1. Communist state--Decision making. I. Douglass, Joseph D. II. Institute for Foreign Policy Analysis. III. Title. IV. Series.
    JC474.S357 1986   321.9′2′068   85-31994
    ISBN 0-08-033651-5 (pbk.)

Printed in the United States of America

Contents

Foreword v

Summary Overview ix

1. Communist Organizational Principles and Ideology 1
   Dictatorship of the Proletariat 1
   Party Unity and Discipline 5
   Democratic Centralism 6
   Ideology 7

2. Party Decision-Making Bodies 9
   The Party Congress 9
   The Central Committee 14
   The Departments 17
   The Secretariats 20
   The Politburo 23

3. Government and National Assembly 25

4. Military Decision-Making 30
   The Defense Council 30
   The Ministry of Defense 40

5. Communist Planning Process 46
   One-Year Plans 46
   Five-Year Plans 47
   Long-Range Plans 48
   The Operation Plan 50
   Preparing the Operation Plan 54
   Material Technical Supply Plan 57
   Mobilization Plan 58

6. Control and Oversight 60
   Personnel and Career Progression 60
   Nomenklatura 61
   Decision Implementation Oversight 64

7. **Case Studies of Decision-Making** 67
   Deployment of Anti-Aircraft Missiles into Czechoslovakia
   in the Early 1960s................................... 67
   The Shift from Defense to Offense in 1963 69
   The Militarization of Society in the mid-1960s 71
   The Process of Converting Castro's Cuba into a Marxist-
   Leninist State 72

Foreword

On February 25, 1968, General Major Jan Sejna left Czechoslovakia and requested political asylum in the United States. Sejna is believed to be the only Communist Party official ever to defect to the West who had served inside the decision-making process of his country's government at the highest level.

Sejna joined the Communist Party of Czechoslovakia in 1946 following World War II. In 1950, he was drafted into the army where, because of his Party background and training, he was made a political officer, or commissar. He rose rapidly through the ranks, a reflection of his own natural ability, drive, and hard work, and the shortage of leadership within the working class. By the age of 27 he was a colonel, a member of parliament, and a member of the Central Committee of the Communist Party of Czechoslovakia.

From 1956 until his defection in 1968, he operated at the center of power in Czechoslovakia. A listing of the various positions he held after 1954, most of them continuously until 1968, provides clear evidence of his experience in and knowledge of the internal workings of the communist decision-making process at the highest level:

1954
- Member of the Central Committee
- Member of the National Assembly

1956
- Chief of Staff to the Minister of Defense, also referred to as Chief of Cabinet
- Secretary of the Military Committee of the Central Committee, retitled the Defense Council in 1969

1964
- Member of the Presidium of the National Assembly
- Member of the Presidium Party Group
- First Secretary of the Main Party Committee at the Ministry of Defense
- Member of the Military Section of the Administration Department
- Member of the Bureau of the Main Political Administration
- Member of the Kolegium of the Minister of Defense

Additionally, he headed and served on numerous committees while acting in the above capacities. Of all these activities, unquestionably the most significant was that of Secretary of the Defense Council. As will be described, the Defense Council is the most important decision-making body in the fields of foreign policy, intelligence, military affairs, and, in several respects, even the economy and industry.

In this monograph, Sejna takes the reader inside the communist decision-making apparatus and explains how it actually works. His account is especially noteworthy not just because of his own experience and knowledge, but because it is written with an appreciation of the manner in which the communist decision-making apparatus is often misunderstood in the West.

The focus is on decision-making in Czechoslovakia during the 1960s. At the same time, Senja provides numerous insights regarding the Soviet system, because in his various capacities he was regularly involved with the top Soviet leadership and Soviet organizations. From 1955 until his departure in 1968, Sejna was in daily contact with his Soviet advisers, spent more than two months each year in the Soviet Union and countless thousands of hours in meetings and informal discussions with the Soviet strategic leadership and with officials in the Party and military apparatus. His task was to understand the Soviet system in operation to ensure that Czechoslovakia evolved in a like manner and supported Soviet objectives. As a result, he came to understand quite well the manner in which both systems operated, their similarities and, occasionally, differences.

It is the similarities among the various communist systems that make this book so important for an understanding of communist decision-making as a whole rather than just decision-making in Czechoslovakia. The forte of Soviet communism is a combination of ideology and organization. As communists move into other countries, this basic organization and ideology is duplicated. Consequently, the organization and operation that one finds in Czechoslovakia will be very similar to that in East Germany, Poland, Rumania, and even Cuba for that matter. There are subtle differences. Occasionally organizations have different names, and where there have been strong internal factions or personalities, such as Castro in Cuba, it takes a while for the organization to be molded into the Soviet image. Ultimately, however, the objective is duplicate organization, process, and ideology. Understanding how the decision-making process works in Czechoslovakia can take one a long way toward understanding how that same process works in the Soviet Union and in Cuba.

While the organizations do change and shift through the years, such changes tend to be ones of form rather than function. Organizations may shift locations on organizational charts or have their names altered, often for purposes of deception, and new ones are chartered when appropriate, but the basic functions continue and the manner in which the system operates today will not be significantly different from what it was in the 1960s. This can be seen in a variety of studies that trace the evolution of specific entities, such as the Defense Council, the secret police, internal border troops, the ministries, and other government bodies. The names change, sometimes organizations split and may or may not come back together, but the basic functions continue. For example, the origins of the Czechoslovak Defense

Council can be seen first in the *Trojka* and, later, in the Military Committee of the Central Committee of the Communist Party, before it formally was redesignated the Defense Council, or, more formally, the Highest Council of the Defense of the State, in 1969. And in 1969, the title of the head of the Party was changed from First Secretary to Secretary General. Also, while in the 1960s the Secretariat of the Czechoslovak Defense Council was headed by a political officer, its function and process remained the same in the 1970s when the Secretariat came under the Chief of the General Staff. This is where the Secretariat is normally placed; however, this practice had not been followed early in the evolution of the Czechoslovak system simply because of the bourgeois background of the Chief of the Czechoslovak General Staff and Soviet concern over his ideological reliability.

Throughout this study, the more recent designators, i.e., Defense Council and Secretary General, will be used even though they were not in use when Sejna held his positions. Additionally, some positions and organizations are referred to by the more common Western or Soviet designators, to avoid confusion: for example, the Chairman of the Council of Ministers is referred to as the Prime Minister, and the Foreign Department is referred to as the International Department.

This study represents Jan Sejna's interpretation of how the system works, expressed in as simple and direct terms as is possible.

Joseph D. Douglass, Jr.
McLean, Virginia

Summary Overview

Jan Sejna is the only known high-ranking Communist Party official with access to the top decision-making process to have defected to the West. From 1956 until his defection from Czechoslovakia in 1968, General Major Sejna held a variety of Party and government positions, including membership in the Central Committee, the National Assembly, the Presidium of the National Assembly, the Military Section of the Administration Department, the Bureau of the Main Political Administration, and the Kolegium of the Ministry of Defense; he also served as a member of the inner decision-making councils at the Ministry of Defense, Defense Council, Main Political Administration, and National Assembly.

The purpose of this monograph is to take the reader inside the communist decision-making process, as known to one who was there. Throughout, the focus is on Czechoslovakia, but since the Czechoslovak system (and that of every other communist system) is closely patterned after that of the Soviet Union, the author's comments apply equally to the Soviet system—and, for example, to the East German and Cuban systems.

Sejna explains how basic communist principles, such as the dictatorship of the proletariat, party unity and discipline, and democratic centralism, serve as effective tools of totalitarian power, and how the Communist Party elites use these tools to retain and exercise power. He describes how the system actually operates, as opposed to the image often projected. In the process, numerous critical insights are provided, many of which clash with prevalent Western perceptions.

In the communist system, the State is the collection of instruments of Party power—military forces, secret police, system of justice, government bureaucrats, etc. Through the State, the Party elite controls the nation and all decision-making processes.

Communist ideology is definitely not dead, as many in the West are prone to believe—or hope. Rather, it is alive and well and functioning, an integral part of the communist system in operation. Ideology defines the content and objectives that guide and shape Party actions, programs, and decisions. It is the basis for party unity and the key to discipline.

The principle of party unity means that all members support the ideological and political line and are fully in accord with Party decisions, which are carefully coordinated in advance to assure that unanimity exists or can be attained when issues are presented for decision. Disagreement exists within the communist system, but it is not expressed openly, because in straying from the path of unity one risks being expelled from the Party, and losing one's career.

Party discipline is used to enforce unity. Anyone who tries to disrupt Party unity is labeled an instrument of capitalism and is, therefore, a criminal subject to punishment. The Party is a militant organization that does not tolerate any fractions or minority points of view. Guidelines and decisions are formulated at the top and passed down to subordinates.

Absolutely crucial to the communist system is the role of deception. It is endemic in all Leninist practices and procedures; without it, the ideology, party control, strategy and tactics, the system as a whole, would be severely weakened. Communism as a political system is difficult for people in the West to comprehend, because Western political systems are not founded on deception—whereas the very mortar of Leninism is deception.

Democratic centralism is one of the major deceptions. In the communist system, everything is pre-arranged, especially "elections." A very small minority, the Party elite, governs. This is the essence of dictatorship; nothing can be left to chance. Everything is tightly orchestrated, from elections and planning processes to decision-making.

The decision-making power in the communist system resides in the Party, whose preeminent leader is the Secretary General. He derives power and influence—not from any *government* post—but from his position as chairman of the critical *Party* organs: the Central Committee, the Politburo, the "Elected" Secretariat (where the power of the Party bureaucracy resides), and the Defense Council (which is dominant in questions of defense, intelligence, and national security).

Along with the Secretary General, the departments and secretariats of the Party are the real power centers of the communist system. Within each department are sections that correspond to and control the various ministries and other government bodies. While the ministers are the government officials, responsible under the Constitution for their respective areas, the real power and control is in the Party's departments, not the government ministries. Department and section heads are, in reality, better informed as well as more powerful than the heads of the ministries they control. Within each ministry—such as the Ministry of Defense—there is a First Secretary of the Party. (Sejna was the First Secretary at the Czechoslovak Ministry of Defense.) It is the responsibility of the First Secretary to keep the controlling section of the cognizant Party department—in Sejna's case the Military Section of the Party's Administration Department—informed about the activities and performance of that ministry.

The four most important Party departments are Administration, Party Organization, Ideology, and International (foreign affairs). The Administration Department, for example, controls the Ministry of Defense, Ministry of Interior (secret police), Ministry of Justice, and other defense organizations.

From the decision-making point of view, the three key organizations are the Defense Council, the Elected Secretariat, and the Politburo. The Defense Council is the highest-level decision-making body in Soviet communist systems, with responsibility for military affairs, intelligence, counter-intelligence, foreign policy, economics, and industry. Anything that can affect the progress of socialism, at home and abroad, is the province of the Defense Council. It makes decisions on collective security arrangements, military strategy and tactics, strategic deception, and all plans and preparations for the conduct of war. The Secretary General is Chairman of the Council, and his deputy is also the Council's Deputy Chairman. Its other members, by law, are the Prime Minister, the Minister of Interior, Chief of the State Planning Commission, and the Minister of Defense.

The Elected Secretariat, also chaired by the Secretary General, is composed of the secretaries, some of whom head the powerful Party departments and others supervise the operations of several departments. They are also, by law, members of the Party's Central Committee. The duties of this Secretariat include organizing the day-to-day work of the Party machinery; issuing directives to the press, propaganda agencies, and mass organizations regarding the Party "line"; appointing key officials to many important posts in such areas as the press and scientific and cultural organizations; making policy decisions regarding censorship and deception; and directing Party work in the armed forces.

The Politburo, headed by the Secretary General, is composed mainly of the leading Party bureaucrats, as well as the most important secretaries of the Central Committees of the republics, the first secretaries of selected regions, and several of the most important government ministers (for example, the Prime Minister, Chairman of the State Planning Commission, Minister of Defense, Foreign Minister, and Interior Minister). The Politburo is concerned primarily with economic and social issues, short-term plans, new laws to be submitted to parliament, and some foreign policy issues. It does not discuss top secret defense and intelligence matters.

While many people recognize that the communist system is a highly centralized and planned society, there is little appreciation of the extent and importance of the planning that actually takes place.

One-year plans are prepared in the summer and fall and generally run from January through December. These plans are approved at the Politburo level and monitored by all the departments. Five-year plans lay out the integrated political, military, and economic strategy. These plans are developed by a team of experts from all departments and critical institutions, e.g., the Science Academy. This planning process is roughly a two-year effort that, since the mid-1950s, has been coordinated with the five-year economic budget and Party Congress.

Long-range plans that extend 15 years and beyond set forth global strategy. This type of plan differs from the one- and five-year plans in that it is broader in scope, sets the overall strategy, and establishes goals, tactics, and areas of responsibilities; but it does not spell out detailed plans and responsibilities.

All of these plans are of vital importance. They are not mere paper exercises. As they are developed, the means of implementation and control are also designed and concurrently approved to ensure that the plans are both realistic and meaningful and that they are, indeed, carried out.

In presenting this material, Sejna has included a variety of examples that illustrate how the communist system works. Of particular interest are lists of topics addressed by the Defense Council, the specific coverage of the long-range plan as it was developed in 1967-1969, the system of *nomenklatura* and related power of appointment, and the process whereby Cuba was turned into a Soviet surrogate.

1.
Communist Organizational Principles and Ideology

WHEN LENIN TOOK power in 1917, he set forth a variety of principles for the "party of the new type," which he called the Communist Party. It is essential to understand these principles and the basic concept and role of ideology in order to appreciate the manner in which the decision-making process operates in the Soviet Union and other communist countries.

These principles—the dictatorship of the proletariat, party unity and discipline, and democratic centralism—and ideology are deceptively simple. But it is their simplicity that makes them effective as the tools of power—totalitarian power. They are the tools with which the top echelons of the Communist Party of the Soviet Union retain and exercise power.

In addition to simplicity, they share the pervasive characteristic of deception. Above all, the communist system is built on a base of deception, which those in power well recognize. Thus, the dictatorship of the proletariat is really dictatorship over the proletariat. The revolution of the proletariat is a revolution of a minority. Party unity is not unanimity of opinion or belief but unity of action and expression enforced from above. Democratic centralism has nothing to do with the democratic process, except in appearance, in the same sense that the government itself is a sham as the concept of government is understood in the West. The Marxist-Leninist ideology is neither communist nor Marxist. It is strictly Leninism couched in the rhetoric of Marx to add a patina of respectability.

Most significant of all, and illustrative of the whole, is the concept of State. In the Soviet Union and throughout the satellites, the State is the collection of instruments of Party power—military forces, regular and secret police, justice system, and government bureaucrats. The State is the means whereby the Party maintains control. The State represents the power of the Party—the Party elite. Through the State, the Party elite controls the nation and all its processes. These processes exist and are maintained to achieve the strategic goals of the Party. This is the essence of so-called communism.

Dictatorship of the Proletariat

The most appropriate point of departure is the dictatorship of the proletariat. Knowing what this concept means and how it operates, including

1

its inherent deceptive nature, is one of the most fundamental keys to an understanding of communism.

The dictatorship begins with the revolution of the proletariat. While this revolution depends to a certain extent on the proletariat and is conducted in its name, the revolution is neither for nor by the proletariat. Nor is the dictatorship of the proletariat controlled by the proletariat. The revolution is the product of a very few, a small minority; its purpose is to seize power, to erect the dictatorship. The enemy, that is, those who would challenge and obstruct the process, are the people of power and means—the capitalists—and the "system." The object of the revolution is to crush all opposition; the old system of government is to be destroyed and a new system created. Thus, the main enemy or obstacle to be overcome, i.e., destroyed, is capitalism—and private ownership. Economic power is to be taken from the bourgeoisie and everything that might lead to the regeneration of capitalism is to be liquidated. The entire state apparatus, which in Marxist language means the government, military forces, and police forces, is to be wiped out. The revolution must consist of a *new* class managing with *new* machinery, as Lenin repeatedly stated.

Marxism-Leninism teaches that immediately after the revolution, the first task is to nationalize banks and insurance companies, and, second, private companies or means of production. Banks and insurance companies come first because of the leverage they hold over the private sector. Thus, the communists make full use of the capitalist system in the process of destroying that system. This task must be performed gradually and with skill because, as the communists recognize, people will not voluntarily give up their property, their businesses, or their farms. Political organization work—the use of all instruments from propaganda and agitation to jails, for the purpose of liquidating the private sector—comes into play at this point.

A good example of political organization work is the program for nationalizing property. A specific rate of collectivization to be achieved is first established. In Czechoslovakia, the tactic devised to maintain this rate—following the nationalization of large farms (over 100 acres)—was to have every second small farmer or owner of a small shop "go to socialization through jail." What this means is that the state would set taxes so high that they could not be paid, and production quotas so high that they could not be fulfilled. The shop or farm owner would be arrested for failing to meet his obligations and would face a long jail term. As an alternative, he would be offered the opportunity to sign over his property to collectivization and go free—an option most people readily accepted. This is political organization work in practice.

In 1951, this political organization work was proceeding at a snail's pace in Czechoslovakia. The Soviet Politburo expressed its displeasure with this situation and summoned the top leadership to Moscow. Voroshilov, a member of the Politburo, was assigned the task of meeting with and disciplining the Czechoslovak leaders. At that time, all Soviet officials were working hard to "out-Stalin" Stalin. If Stalin said something was bad, his lieutenants would say it was atrocious. Voroshilov severely criticized the Czechoslovaks, and, upon returning home, they greatly accelerated the process.

First, the remaining middle-size farms (30 to 100 acres) were confiscated. Key individuals were accused of crimes, arrested, and sentenced to jail for twenty years or so; their houses and property then were taken over. During the night, the military would take trucks, arrest the influential bourgeoisie, including farmers, evict them from their houses, apartments, and lands, and move them far from their neighborhoods to places where they would have no power. These were the people who had exercised major influence in the villages and towns, so the communists had to move them out before strong nationalization and collectivization pressure could be applied. Large farms were broken up and given to the people with the slogan, "The land belongs to those who work on it." Two years later, these small farms were turned into collective farms, and the communists told the people that their land was not being taken from them but was merely being consolidated so that they could all work together and benefit from better technology. The granting of rights and privileges and the imposition of penalties—hunting permits, motorcycle permits, taxes, police arrests (usually before Christmas)—were orchestrated to speed the process. No one hesitated for more than three days before signing over his farm to collectivization, and by 1954 the process had been completed. The means used—military, police, courts, laws—are referred to collectively as "political means," and the process as political organization work.

An aspect of this that is rarely fully appreciated in the West is the role of deception. The land is appropriated to be turned over "to the people," and then the land is "voluntarily" turned over to collectivization—and, of course, the unspoken alternative is jail. The people are allowed to work "their" land, but all this is deception, or lies, whatever one prefers to call it. Deception is endemic in all Leninist practices and procedures, as will be seen throughout these pages. Communism is difficult for the West to understand, because the West does not think in terms of deception—while the very mortar of Leninism is deception.

The deception of communism is perhaps no more clearly apparent than in the basic concept of the dictatorship of the proletariat, which is used to convey the idea that power resides in the working class, i.e., the proletariat. The "people" run the country, the people being the proletariat. But, in reality, all power is wielded by a small minority—the Communist Party. Generally only 5 to 10 percent of the population can aspire to Party membership, and then only after they have been schooled, found to be correctly oriented to the ideology, and "elected" to be members. If they do not support the

Party line, they are "elected" out. The dictatorship of the proletariat justifies the acquisition of all power in the country by an elite minority, the Party leadership. The power used to enforce the dictatorship of the proletariat includes the secret police (the StB in Czechoslovakia, which is the KGB counterpart), the military forces, the press and propaganda apparatus, the courts of justice, the *nomenklatura*[1] (a system of control over positions and career advancement), and the Party Control and Discipline Committee. All of these and other forces are employed to conduct political organization work and carry out "the will of the proletariat."

In the constitutions of all communist countries, the Communist Party is said to represent the leading force of society because it plays the decisive or determining role. This determining role has two sides. First, the Party establishes the ideology and political goals that guide the nation. Second, the Party ensures that the goals are implemented. This second aspect is critical; implementation is closely tied to formulation. Political goals and ideology are not just idle statements: when they are set by the Party, a plan and an organization are established to achieve the goals and ensure that the ideology is implemented. This is also true in the case of the decision-making process. When a decision is made, the plan and organization by which it is to be carried out is set forth from top to bottom—as part of that decision. In the broadest sense, through the state and political mechanisms, the Party organizes the society to achieve the goals. In Marxist language, the ideology and the political organization work of the Party are *united*.

The organization of power is one of the strong points of the communist system. Communists are masters at organization and tactics. By organization is meant not merely the development of flow charts or organizational manuals or the assignment of goals and purpose, but, equally important, the tactics to achieve the goals in an orderly fashion. Communism is an active, not a passive, ideology, and this is reflected in the approach to organization. Organization means militant control and active use from top to bottom of all the instruments of power in support of Party goals, ideology, and plans.

Unfortunately, the common tendency in the West is to dismiss what the communists say, for example at Party Congresses, as mere propaganda or rhetoric. This is very dangerous because, where goals are stated and ideology is set forth by communist leaders, you can be assured there is a plan and an organization already established and working to achieve those goals and implement the ideology. Ideology is not enunciated just for the sake of having an ideology. Ideology justifies the goals and the strategy. It is an active and powerful force.

Moreover, in the global communist movement, only the Soviet Union has the right to decide what is Marxist and to set the strategic goals. When

---

[1] See Chapter 6 for a more complete description.

Soviet Party leaders present the "Party line," it is, by definition, the Marxist line that all countries and foreign communist parties are obliged to follow and put into practice. In the case of the satellite countries, it is generally easy for the Soviet Union to enforce this process because the Soviets control the centers of power within the various Warsaw Pact countries. In the international communist movement, however, it is more difficult to enforce because the Soviet Union cannot always wield power over farflung communist parties. In these cases, the Kremlin's main tools are those of conspiracy, blackmail, bribery, and, most of all, deception.

Party Unity and Discipline

When votes taken in a Party Congress, the parliament, and other bodies are announced, they are described as 100 percent favorable or unanimous votes. This is not an example of happenstance or unbridled enthusiasm; rather, it results from the principle of Party unity and discipline.

The principle of Party unity means that all members are working for the Party, support the ideology and political line, and are fully in accord with and support Party decisions, which are carefully coordinated in advance to assure that unanimity exists or can be attained when issues are presented for decision. But this is an artificial unity. There is disagreement in the communist system, perhaps as much as anywhere else; it simply is not expressed, or is very carefully couched, because in straying from the path of unity one risks being expelled from the Party. The time when disagreements surface is in the midst of a crisis, when there is not enough time to establish Party positions in advance. In this case, the key to success —often even to survival—is judging which side of the disagreement will win out in the end, and being on that side at the end.

Party discipline is used to enforce unity. Anyone who tries to disrupt the unity of the Party is labeled an instrument of capitalism and is, therefore, by definition, a criminal subject to punishment. The Party is a militant organization that does not tolerate any fractions or minority points of view. Principles and decisions are formulated at the top and passed down to subordinates. All such decisions must be followed by all members, and anyone who does not, is an enemy of the Party. The role of the Party Control and Revision Commission is to examine these enemies and decide how guilty they are and mete out the appropriate punishment. Party Control and Revision Commissions exist from the regional level up to the Central Committee; in the military forces, they exist from division up to the Ministry of Defense.

Accusing an individual of breaking Party unity is one of the major weapons by which the Party leadership controls the members. To be accused of breaking unity is to be branded an enemy. Examples are easy to find: Khrushchev, in the process of consolidating his power, accused Molotov and Malenkov of conspiring to break Party unity. In Czechoslovakia, the Minister of the Interior, that is, the minister in charge of internal security, Rudolf Barak, who was also a member of the Politburo, was arrested and placed in jail. At the next meeting of the Central Committee, it was decided to oust him from the Party. The Minister of Finance, Julis Duris, stood up and asked why the Minister of the Interior was not present, and he, too, was fired for disturbing Party unity.

Democratic Centralism

Democratic centralism in Marxist language means in theory that all Party bodies are elected from the bottom up and afterward all decisions flow from the top down. On the surface, this appears to be quite democratic to the Western observer. However, this is mainly a deception because in the communist system nothing is left to chance. Everything is pre-arranged, including the elections. The unspoken rationale is quite well recognized at the top. It is a very small minority that governs. This is the essence of the dictatorship, and this is why nothing can be left to chance. That is, one cannot afford to leave any opening for the enemy. As recently explained by a member of the CPSU Central Committee, "Any deviation from the principles of democratic centralism is, as experience has shown, fraught with the danger of considerable loss."

Hence, while the notion is that Party bodies are elected from the bottom up, actually the election process is determined from the top down. For example, in 1954, the District First Secretary told Jan Sejna he had received orders from the Central Committee that Sejna was to be elected to the District Conference of the Party, nominated to the Regional Party Conference, chosen as a delegate to the 10th Party Congress, and then elected to the Central Committee of the Communist Party of Czechoslovakia. Being a low-level political officer in an engineer brigade, and going to the Party Congress for the first time, Sejna was astonished at the idea that anyone could vote for him for anything. He was totally unknown, even at the regional level. Nonetheless, he was elected—unanimously. Later, when he asked what he was expected to do as a member of the Central Committee, he was told to "Do nothing. Just attend the meetings, sit and listen, and vote when called upon." A couple of weeks later, the Secretary General himself telephoned to inform him that he would be elected to the National Assembly. The Politburo had decided. This time he was less astonished when the prediction came true—again, unanimously.

Everything is orchestrated. Even the "free discussion" at various Party organizational levels is orchestrated from the top down. Discussion leaders are provided guidelines on what they are to say and what their subordinates may say and what topics may be considered. If the discussion deviates from the desired direction, those responsible will face disciplinary action for breaking Party unity.

Ideology

Ideology, one of the most important elements in the communist system, is defined in communist texts as a system of political, legal, scientific, philosophical, religious, ethical, and aesthetic ideas and views. The Soviet ideology is called Marxism-Leninism.

In the West the communist ideology is one of the most misrepresented and poorly understood elements of the communist system. The common view is that communist ideology is dead, that nobody believes in it any more. Such statements are made by many eminent Sovietologists, defectors, and émigrés. Again, however, there is confusion over words and what is really meant when one says that the ideology is dead. Usually what people mean is that Marxism-Leninism is no longer regarded as infallible, or that communism is not the Utopia it was advertised to be in the early part of this century. In this sense, there is considerable truth to the statement that the ideology is dead—the visions and the theories are bankrupt—where the communists are fully in control.

As you move up the system and grow to understand it, you also begin to recognize that many integral parts of the system are part of the deception, including aspects of the visions and theories. For example, Marxism is used to design the tactical steps to take in the transition to communism, and most of these are deceptions. Foremost among these deceptions is the use of terms such as communism and Marxism. The strategic goals of the Soviet Union and communism are different, and the ideology is not really Marxism. Marxism, communism, and socialism are exploited by the Soviet Union in the quest for power. The Marxist-Leninist ideology is the sales pitch, the "sugar that makes the medicine go down." The target audience is the people, the working class, the uncommitted and unsuspecting, the poor and uneducated, as well as the intellectual middle class. By the time they understand what is happening, that they have been deceived, it is too late because the controls, i.e., the dictatorship of the proletariat, have been established, and they are trapped. But the ideology that governs Soviet actions and policies is alive and well, and ready to be used against the next unsuspecting or vulnerable target country.

Another way in which ideology is used is through *internal* Party operations in the Soviet Union and other countries taken over by the Soviets. As employed internally, ideology defines the content, aims, and objectives that guide and shape Party actions, programs, and decisions. It determines how Party members are allowed to think. Used in this sense, communist ideology remains the primary force. It is the basis for Party unity, the guideline for action, and the key to discipline. This latter point is most important: If you are not aligned with the ideology, you face expulsion from the Party and your career, your opportunity to advance, is ended.

Ideology is not fixed and rigid; it changes to keep pace with the times, to justify communist goals, strategy, and tactics. The explanation of the need for such changes is simple: Lenin could see only so far into the future. (However, only Moscow can admit this.) The main lines, however, have not changed. The primary goals remain: to destroy capitalism, starting with the largest elements, which is why the United States is the main enemy; to dominate all Third World countries; to make the Soviet Union the strongest military power in the world; and to liquidate all religion. The liquidation of religion is essential because there can be no higher authority (i.e., God) than the Party. Communism itself is a militant religion with its own ideological beliefs and commandments, which are no less powerful and compelling to the faithful today than the teachings of Christ, Buddha, Mohammed, or Moses.

2.
Party Decision-Making Bodies

THE DECISION-MAKING power in the communist system resides in the Party. The head of the Party, the preeminent leader, is the Secretary General, who derives his power and influence from his position as chairman of the critical Party organizations: the Central Committee; the Politburo; the Secretariat, where the real power of the Party bureaucracy resides; and the Defense Council, which is dominant in questions of defense, intelligence, and national security.

The most important Party organizations are shown in Figure 1. This chart also illustrates selected portions of the functional control wielded by the various secretaries and Party departments both through the Party organizations arrayed on the left side of verticle lines under the departments and also through the government organizations (e.g., ministries) arrayed on the right side. The main difference between Czechoslovak and Soviet organizations is size. A Soviet chart will show several organizations which are combined into one in Czechoslovakia—for example, the Secretary for Ideology and Foreign Policy. A second difference is that Czechoslovakia does not have organizations whose function is to control foreign communist parties. These types of organizations are unique to the Soviet Union.

The Party Congress

The regular Party Congress meets only once every five years. Because it is mainly for display purposes and does not wield any power, it was not included in Figure 1. A description of its role does, however, provide a valuable insight into the manner in which the communist system operates.

The Party Congress is the highest *official* Party organization. Since 1956, the Party Congress has been scheduled to coincide with the adoption of the important five-year plan. Its apparent purpose is, indeed, to approve that plan and, in so doing, to ratify and legitimize strategy for the next five years and beyond. This is the major task of the Congress and the focus of most speeches and discussion. Its other important tasks are, under the pretense of "elections," to confirm the selection of new members of the Central Committee and the Control and Revision Commission.

Marxism is difficult to understand because of the deceptive manner in which words and concepts are used. It is considerably different in practice

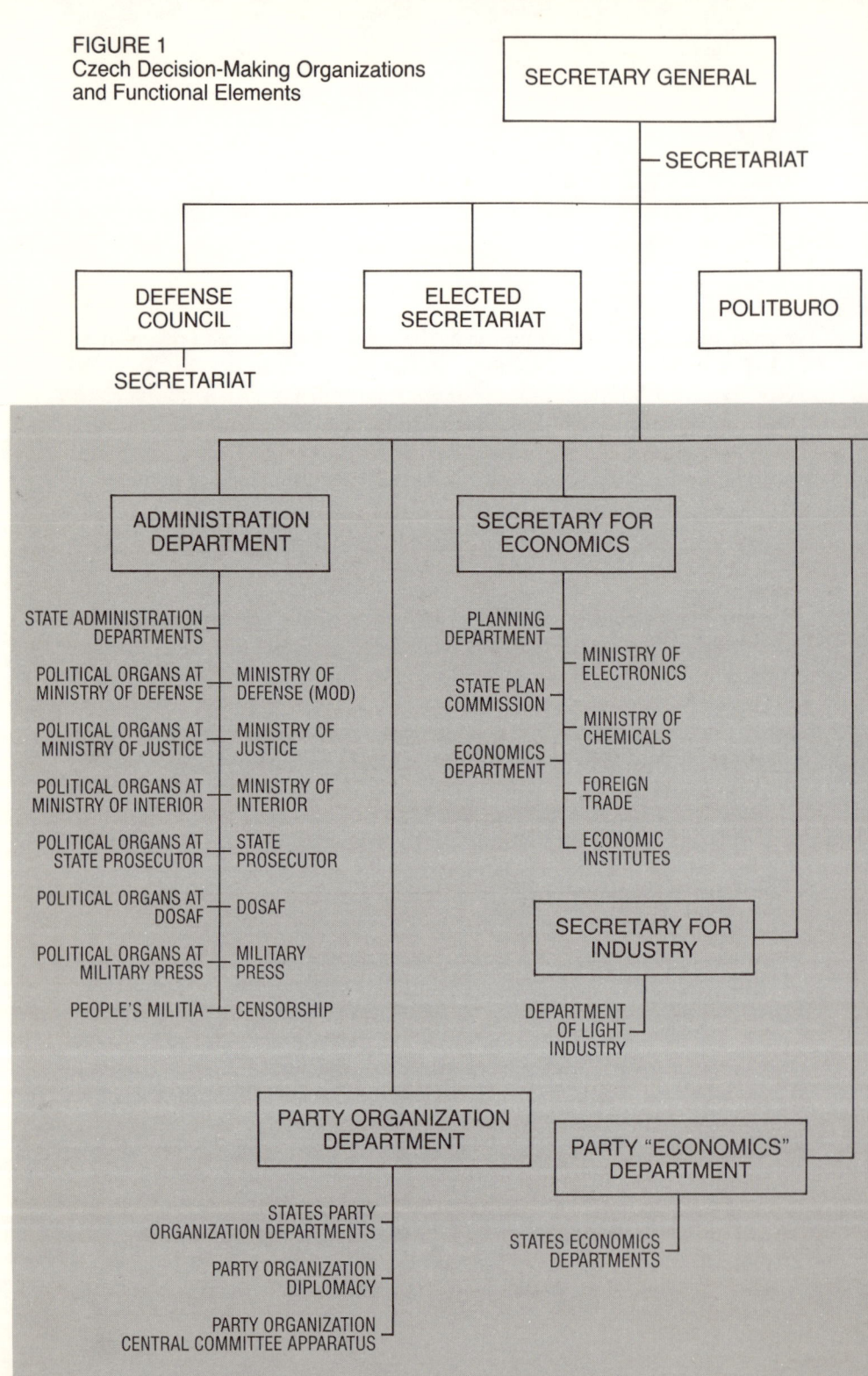

FIGURE 1
Czech Decision-Making Organizations and Functional Elements

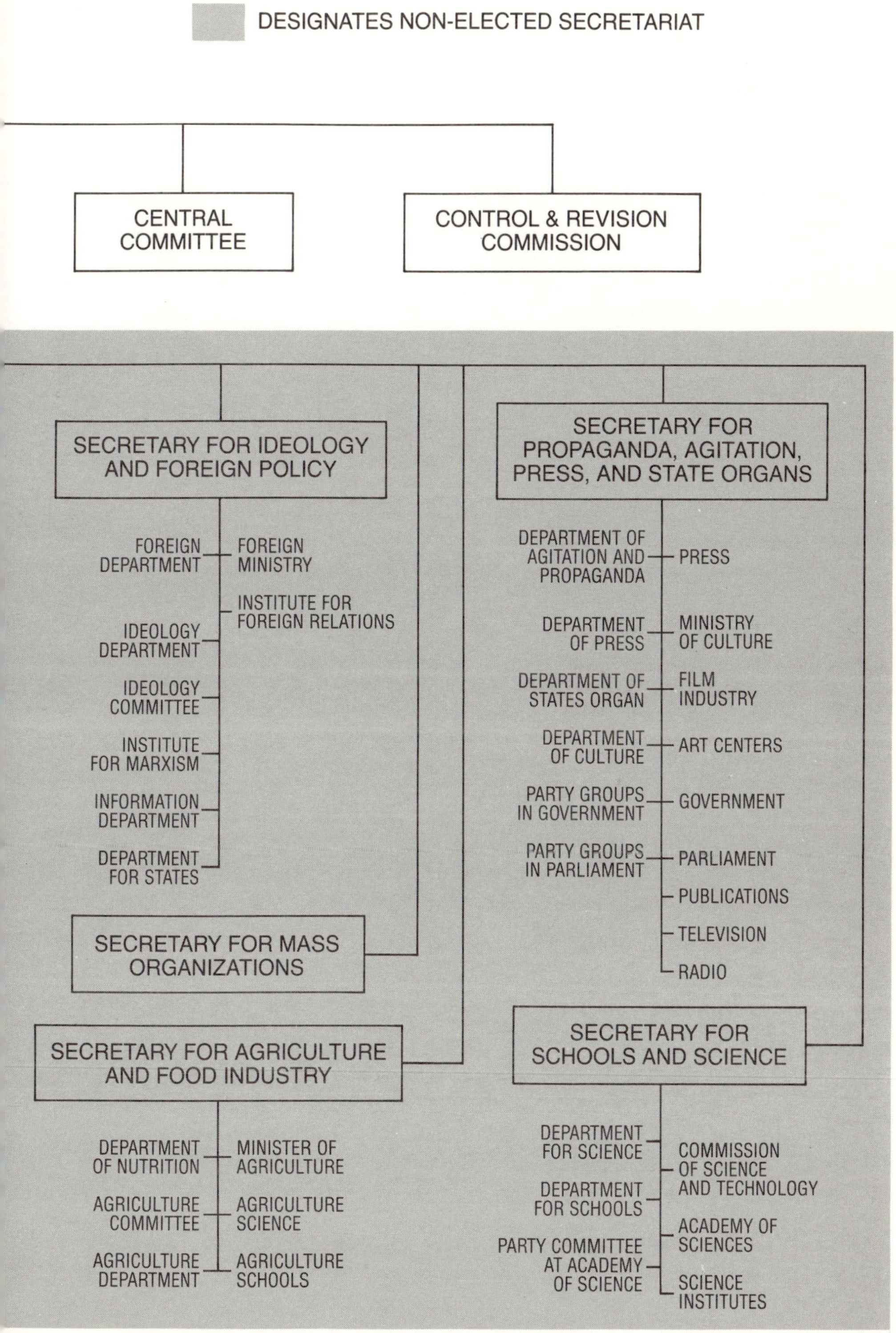

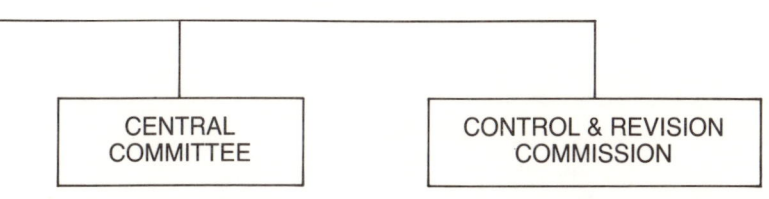

DESIGNATES NON-ELECTED SECRETARIAT

CENTRAL COMMITTEE

CONTROL & REVISION COMMISSION

SECRETARY FOR IDEOLOGY AND FOREIGN POLICY

- FOREIGN DEPARTMENT — FOREIGN MINISTRY
  - INSTITUTE FOR FOREIGN RELATIONS
- IDEOLOGY DEPARTMENT
- IDEOLOGY COMMITTEE
- INSTITUTE FOR MARXISM
- INFORMATION DEPARTMENT
- DEPARTMENT FOR STATES

SECRETARY FOR PROPAGANDA, AGITATION, PRESS, AND STATE ORGANS

- DEPARTMENT OF AGITATION AND PROPAGANDA — PRESS
- DEPARTMENT OF PRESS — MINISTRY OF CULTURE
- DEPARTMENT OF STATES ORGAN — FILM INDUSTRY
- DEPARTMENT OF CULTURE — ART CENTERS
- PARTY GROUPS IN GOVERNMENT — GOVERNMENT
- PARTY GROUPS IN PARLIAMENT — PARLIAMENT
  - PUBLICATIONS
  - TELEVISION
  - RADIO

SECRETARY FOR MASS ORGANIZATIONS

SECRETARY FOR AGRICULTURE AND FOOD INDUSTRY

- DEPARTMENT OF NUTRITION — MINISTER OF AGRICULTURE
- AGRICULTURE COMMITTEE — AGRICULTURE SCIENCE
- AGRICULTURE DEPARTMENT — AGRICULTURE SCHOOLS

SECRETARY FOR SCHOOLS AND SCIENCE

- DEPARTMENT FOR SCIENCE — COMMISSION OF SCIENCE AND TECHNOLOGY
- DEPARTMENT FOR SCHOOLS — ACADEMY OF SCIENCES
- PARTY COMMITTEE AT ACADEMY OF SCIENCE — SCIENCE INSTITUTES

from theoretical descriptions of how it operates. This is the case with "decisions" and "elections" attributed to the Party Congress.

Preparation for the Party Congress takes two years. A special committee, representing the secretaries of the Central Committee, is appointed by the Politburo to prepare the Congress. In 95 percent of the cases, this special committee is headed by the Deputy Secretary General, which is a de facto rather than de jure position. In the Soviet Union, this deputy is always one of the Central Committee secretaries in whom the Secretary General reposes full trust. His responsibilities are defined by the Secretary General. In Czechoslovakia, the Deputy Secretary General, who was also referred to as the Second Secretary, was usually the secretary in charge of ideology.

The special committee is composed of important secretaries of the Central Committee, heads of important departments of the Central Committee, and leading experts in science, technology, military affairs, and ideology. Numerous subcommittees are formed and attached to the special committee; they usually correspond to the various departments of the Central Committee, that is, to the broad areas around which operations and planning in the communist system are organized. These subcommittees are led by the heads of the corresponding departments, who, in turn, are members of the special committee. The members of the subcommittees are also appointed by the Politburo.

The task of the special committee is to prepare the strategic guidance that the subcommittees will use in preparing detailed plans and programs. This guidance is first submitted to the Politburo, and when it has been approved, it becomes the strategy that is to be followed over the next five years. The subcommittees then receive this guidance, and proceed to draw up plans and programs in the various policy areas and make recommendations on the matters that should be discussed and acted upon by the Party Congress. These recommendations will be reviewed and approved by the Politburo and then used by the Party Organization Department in setting up the Congress and establishing its agenda.

The work of the subcommittees is carefully scheduled over this two-year period to assure an orderly pace for the development of plans and their presentation to the special committee, and thence to the Politburo. In the scheduling, the International Department (Foreign Department) will usually take the lead because its analyses and recommendations cover the world situation; it strives to set forth the overall global strategy that is to be pursued over the next five years, and the role of the various instruments that are to be employed in the implementation of the strategy. Other departments then focus on this strategy in developing their own recommendations for detailed plans and decisions required to carry out the global strategy. All of these plans and programs must eventually be approved by the Party Congress.

In this process, there is one important, unique subcommittee that operates outside the normal approval process and is tightly controlled. This is the subcommittee that represents the interests of the Administration Department, which controls the military, internal security (StB), and justice. The recommendations, plans, and reports of this subcommittee do not go to the special committee or to the Politburo. This subcommittee reports only to the Defense Council, which approves the strategy and detailed plans in these areas. Only a brief general statement of objectives goes to the Politburo and to the Party Congress for approval.

In this manner, all the reports, plans, and decisions are worked out well in advance of the Party Congress *by the Party apparatus*. This is called "Party organization work." Similarly, the Congress itself is orchestrated in advance by the Party apparatus. This is the responsibility of the Party Organization Department, which prepares all aspects of the Party Congress from beginning to end. This department determines how the Congress will be organized, who will be the delegates, who will be elected to the new Central Committee, to the Election Committee, to the Control and Revision Commission, and so forth.

The main work of the Party Organization Department begins six months or more before the Congress is convened—while the various regions are holding their annual Party conferences, at which time they elect representatives to the Republic Party Congresses, which will then elect delegates to attend the Party Congress. This process is strictly controlled by the Party Organization Department down to the regional level to make sure that the right (pre-selected) people and a proper mix of delegates attend the Party Congress. The specified proper mix might include, for example, 20 percent intellectuals, 10 percent women, 50 percent workers, 5 percent military, 5 percent secret police, and 2 percent individuals in culture and the arts—which itself is misleading, because a general who comes from the working class is classified as a worker. When this mix has been approved by the Elected Secretariat, the Party Organization Department instructs the first secretaries of the Party at the republic levels, who head the republics, on the nature of the cross-section that is to come out of each region, which will vary according to the geographic location and demographic characteristics of the regions. The regions recommend names to the Party Organization Department of the Central Committee. Perhaps twice as many names are recommended as will attend, and the lists contain the names that the Party Organization Department has previously instructed the regions to include in the lists. In this manner, the final selection of delegates who attend the Party Congress is strictly controlled by the Party Organization Department. Other departments participate in the selection process with the Party Organization Department to ensure that their respective needs are fulfilled: for example, the Administration Department has an input with regard to military, justice, and secret police delegates; the Agriculture Department, regarding delegates from collective farms, and so forth.

Immediately prior to the Party Congress, the Central Committee meets and approves all major speeches, the selection of cadres who are to be "elected" by the Congress to different committees, and the decisions to be made by the Congress. In short, when the Party Congress convenes, all events have been carefully orchestrated by the Party apparatus.

The Party Congress itself is controlled through the first secretaries of the republics who head their respective delegations. The first secretaries of the regions are instructed in advance as to the issues their delegates should raise for discussion during the Congress and the comments their delegates may offer during the discussions. Thus, the issues raised and the discussions that take place at the Party Congress are controlled in advance through the first secretaries.

The elections at the Congress are administered by the Election Committee, which is usually headed by the Deputy Secretary General. The actual elections are conducted by the Secretary General himself. The manner in which the elections operate can be illustrated by the election of the new Central Committee and of the Control and Revision Commission, which is normally the last action that takes place on the last day of the Congress. After lunch on the last day, when the delegates return to their desks, they find a list of names which have been proposed by the Election Committee for election to the Central Committee and to the Control and Revision Commission. The delegates are given time to read through the list of names, and then a coffee break is called. During the coffee break, should any delegate object to any name, he can raise the matter with the head of his delegation, who in turn will take the objection to the head of the Election Committee. Normally, the head of the Election Committee will simply explain that the objection is inappropriate and that the delegation head should so inform his colleague, which is quickly and forcefully done. After the coffee break is concluded, the election is held, the vote is unanimous, and the Congress is concluded.

The Central Committee

In between meetings of the Party Congress, the Central Committee is the Party body with the highest "official" authority. It responds to the pronouncements of the Party Congress and ensures that its directions are carried out in the intervening years.

The Central Committee meets roughly every other month, or five to six times per year. It is basically a forum to discuss and make recommendations on issues that apply to the whole nation; its deliberations generally adhere to the strict Party policy line. The meetings of the Central Committee are normally not secret; 90 percent are closed, but only those which involve the election of cadres are actually secret. This, in part, explains why discussions in the Central Committee tend to be of a general nature.

The Central Committee issues decisions, provides guidance, and approves major changes in tactics to cope with specific problems that arise. After studying various problems, the Central Committee may direct the Politburo to make general changes. In the case of satellite countries, the Central Committee can also recommend changes to the Soviet Union to resolve specific problems.

As indicated earlier, communist planning and operations are organized around specific subject areas presided over by secretaries of the Central Committee. The operations of each subject area, such as finance and organization, are controlled by departments of the Central Committee, whose heads report to their cognizant secretary. The secretaries of the Party are the most powerful officials in the communist system, and the First Secretary or Secretary General is preeminent. The most powerful organizations are the departments and the Elected Secretariat, the latter being composed of all the secretaries and a few lesser officials such as the Chief Editor of the Party newspaper, which in the Soviet Union is *Pravda*.

As is the case with the Party Congress, meetings of the Central Committee are prepared well in advance. The Elected Secretariat prepares the Central Committee meetings, and in this undertaking the key role is played by the departments. Topics for discussion, speeches, even decisions are prepared in the various departments and submitted to the Elected Secretariat for approval. During this process, each of the Party departments places emphasis on ensuring that its presentations and discussions are very carefully thought out to ensure that any criticism is directed at the government ministries and *not* at the departments. In the communist system, the government takes the blame; the Party takes the credit.

All decisions are carefully reached before meetings. Except in crisis situations, as will be discussed later, all disagreements are resolved in advance and all votes are unanimous. This is another dimension of Party unity: When the issue or decision is formally presented, there is only one view and only one vote, both of which are predetermined. This applies to the Party Congress, as well as to meetings of the Central Committee, Politburo, and Defense Council.

The Central Committee is entitled to review and approve decisions about foreign and domestic policy, the Party, the economy, and the social order. It does not review military policy, except in rare circumstances when a military policy is presented to the Central Committee as a tactic designed to help ensure full Party support for the policy—for example, the military buildup in 1964 on the Sino-Soviet border. The Central Committee does not even discuss military, intelligence, or secret police operations unless there is an unusual crisis, as, for example, in the Soviet Union when Marshal Zhukov was fired.

In preparing meetings of the Central Committee, as in the case of the Party Congress, secret defense and security policy matters are handled only by the Administration Department, which has cognizance over the military, secret police, and justice, and by the Defense Council. The only aspects of defense and security policy matters that are considered by the Elected Secretariat are non-secret matters such as military publications, propaganda, ideology, and daily Party work in the military. Secretaries of the Central Committee and the Politburo who are not members of the Defense Council do not have access to defense and security policy matters, except as the Defense Council decides they have a need to know.

From 1954 to 1968, the Czechoslovak Central Committee discussed military considerations only once (when Cepicka, the Minister of Defense, was fired) and secret policy considerations three times (two involving the "rehabilitation" of innocent people in jail, and once when the Minister of Interior, Barak, was arrested). Intelligence matters were never discussed in the Central Committee. Inside the Soviet Union, military considerations were discussed by the Central Committee when Marshal Zhukov was dismissed; following the increase of Soviet military deployments to the Sino-Soviet border area; and, in general terms, with regard to the ideological indoctrination of the armed forces.

The Central Committee has the power, i.e., nomenklatura, to elect the Secretary General, the secretaries of the Central Committee (which is why the term Elected Secretariat is used to distinguish this secretariat from other secretariats), the ministers, and other government officials. This power of election, however, as in the case of Party Congress elections, amounts to little more than a rubber-stamp operation. Normally, the last item on the agenda of a Central Committee meeting, which usually runs two or three days, is the "Cadres Personnel Questions," on which no prior information has been provided to the Central Committee membership. When all but the last item on the agenda has been completed, there is a coffee break. Following the coffee break, each member is provided a copy of the recommendation of the Politburo on promotions, firings, and appointments that have been prepared by the Party apparatus and approved by the Elected Secretariat. In all cases, the Party apparatus and Elected Secretariat wield the power and make the decisions that are subsequently announced as though the Politburo had made them, when indeed this is not the case. This list of personnel actions is then approved by the Central Committee as the last item on its agenda. Additionally, officials can be appointed and fired in between meetings of the Central Committee, which is asked at its next meeting to approve such actions retroactively.

During his entire career, Sejna can recall only one time when a recommendation on personnel action was challenged by a member of the Central Committee. That instance was in 1956 when Czechoslovak Minister of Defense Cepicka was fired and Lomski was appointed Minister by the Politburo, even though the Minister of Defense was under the nomenklatura of the Central Committee. Roughly three weeks after the appointment, at a meeting of the Central Committee, an old Comintern member, Jan Harus, asked how it was possible for Lomski to have been appointed by the Politburo when the position is under the nomenklatura of the Central Committee, and how was it possible to appoint a Jew to such a high position. Novotny, the First Secretary, stood up and said that it was the Politburo's responsibility to appoint the Minister of Defense because he was needed at his post immediately and therefore it was not possible to wait for a meeting of the Central Committee; second, the Administration Department, together with Soviet comrades from the KGB, had checked many generations back in the Lomski family and had found no Jewish ancestors. There were no further questions.

The Departments

The departments and secretariats of the Party are the real power centers of the communist system. Within each department are sections that correspond to and control the various ministries and other government bodies. While the ministers are the government officials, responsible under the Constitution for their respective areas, the real power and control is in the department sections, not in the ministries.

The heads of the sections are, in reality, better informed and more powerful than the heads of the ministries they control. Within each ministry—such as the Ministry of Defense, the Ministry of Interior (secret police), the Foreign Ministry—there is a First Secretary of the Party. In Czechoslovakia, Sejna was the First Secretary at the Ministry of Defense. It is the responsibility of this First Secretary or chief of the Party body to keep the controlling section of the cognizant department—in Sejna's case the Military Section of the Administration Department—informed about the activities and performance within that ministry.

The principal exception to this general rule is the Operations Administration, which is under the Chief of the General Staff within the General Staff organization. This Administration, as will be discussed later, is responsible for the Operation Plan, which is highly classified and tightly controlled. The only Party organ authorized access to this data is the Defense Council. In this area, the head of the section in the Administration Department that controls the Ministry of Defense has only marginal, indirect knowledge of the operations planning conducted in the Operations Administration.

If he needs to obtain information on the Operation Plan, he must call the Chief of the Operations Department where the planning is conducted within the Administration. This official is the main source of information; other sources are the Party group at the Operations Administration and Operations Department, whose duties include reporting on possible sabotage.

Perhaps the best way to understand what changes are taking place in the Operation Plan, next to contacting the Operations Department, is by observing changes in the Administration of Material and Technical Supply, which is responsible for the technical side of the Operation Plan, an area in which changes are most noticeable. A second area for detecting changes is in the regulations or directions that are issued for troop training during the next year: for example, greatly increased attention to parachute operations, night operations, and offensive operations, as took place in 1964 following the adoption of the new Operation Plan, which implemented a significant shift to offensive, first-strike operations.

From the perspective of the West, knowledge of the workings of several departments, sections, and other internal department organizations is essential to an understanding of the decision process in the communist system.

The four most important departments are Administration, Party Organization, Ideology, and International. The Administration Department controls the Ministry of Defense, Ministry of Interior (secret police), Ministry of Justice, and defense organizations such as DOSAF.[2] The manner in which the Administration Department is structured is shown in Figure 2, and the primary control mechanisms over the Ministry of Defense are shown in Figure 3. The groups under the sections will vary in size according to the complexity or extent of the area. The smallest ones are composed of single individuals and the largest, ten or so. In the Soviet Union these groups are more numerous and larger.

The Party Organization Department controls the Party organs, Party Congresses, Central Committee meetings, and the development of cadres. This department also controls similar departments at the republic and regional levels—a characteristic of all Central Committee departments.

The Ideology Department is especially important, since ideology still plays a major role in establishing direction and guidance for all activities. This department is responsible for developing the philosophy that guides the Party program, and it explains and interprets the Party line. This brings us to one of the more crucial conflicts in the communist system, between theory and practice, or between guidance and implementation. The communist system sorts people into two basic categories: the theoreticians and the organizers. The former are the ideologists and propagandists; they pronounce the Marxist-Leninist principles of development. The latter are the

---

[2] DOSAF is the civilian organization responsible for training the youth for military service and other military needs.

FIGURE 2
Administration Department Organizational Chart

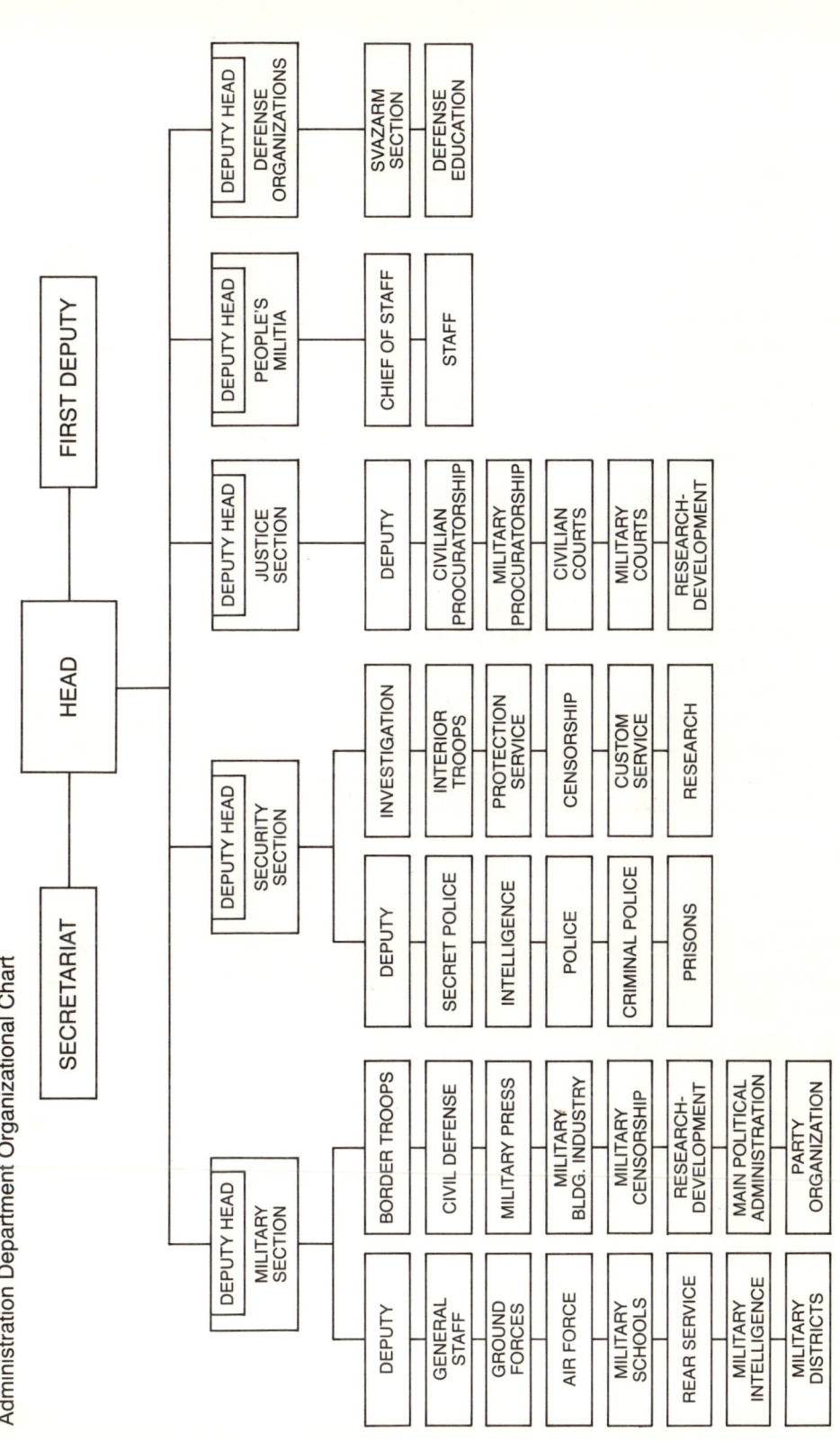

implementors, the practitioners. Each group blames the other for failure to understand its point of view and for being the problem when something goes wrong. These conflicts are strong and continuing.

The International Department, which in Czechoslovakia is called the Foreign Department, is responsible for foreign policy. This department and the Administration Department have the main role and responsibility in the development and implementation of global deception operations. The world revolutionary movement is directed from the Soviet International Department, which receives assistance in this area from the Administration and Press departments. The Press Department controls the media and handles relations with the foreign press. Also involved with information is the International Information Department, which was formed in the late 1960s to integrate information for Party decision-making. Another related department is that of Propaganda Agitation, responsible for mass propaganda and individual influence operations on a large scale—for example, the current peace movement.

Perhaps the least recognized department is a special Party "Economics" Department (there is no good translation for its official name, hence the use of quotes). This department reports directly to the Secretary General and handles Party funds. Each Party member contributes "dues," which are collected by the "Economics" Department and disbursed to pay for Party publications and other matters, including foreign influence operations and foreign communist party finances.

Each Central Committee department has nomenklatura over its own cognizant areas. Nomenklatura for the heads of departments resides in the Politburo. In this case, it is the Party Organization Department that selects the candidates; the respective secretaries then recommend the appointments to the Politburo, which elects (i.e., rubber-stamps) the heads of the departments. Other members of the departments are appointed by the Elected Secretariat.

The Secretariats

In discussing communist decision-making, there are several different secretariats that must be identified. The Secretariat of the Secretary General (in the Soviet Union, this is called the General Department) and the Secretariat of the Chairman of the Defense Council (which is normally a section within the General Staff) are the staffs of those offices. There are also two distinct groups, one large and one small, within Party organizations that are referred to as secretariats: the non-elected Secretariat and the Elected Secretariat. The first, and larger, one is the total collection of the Party bureaucrats who staff the departments and committees that make up the Party organization. These bureaucrats are promoted within their

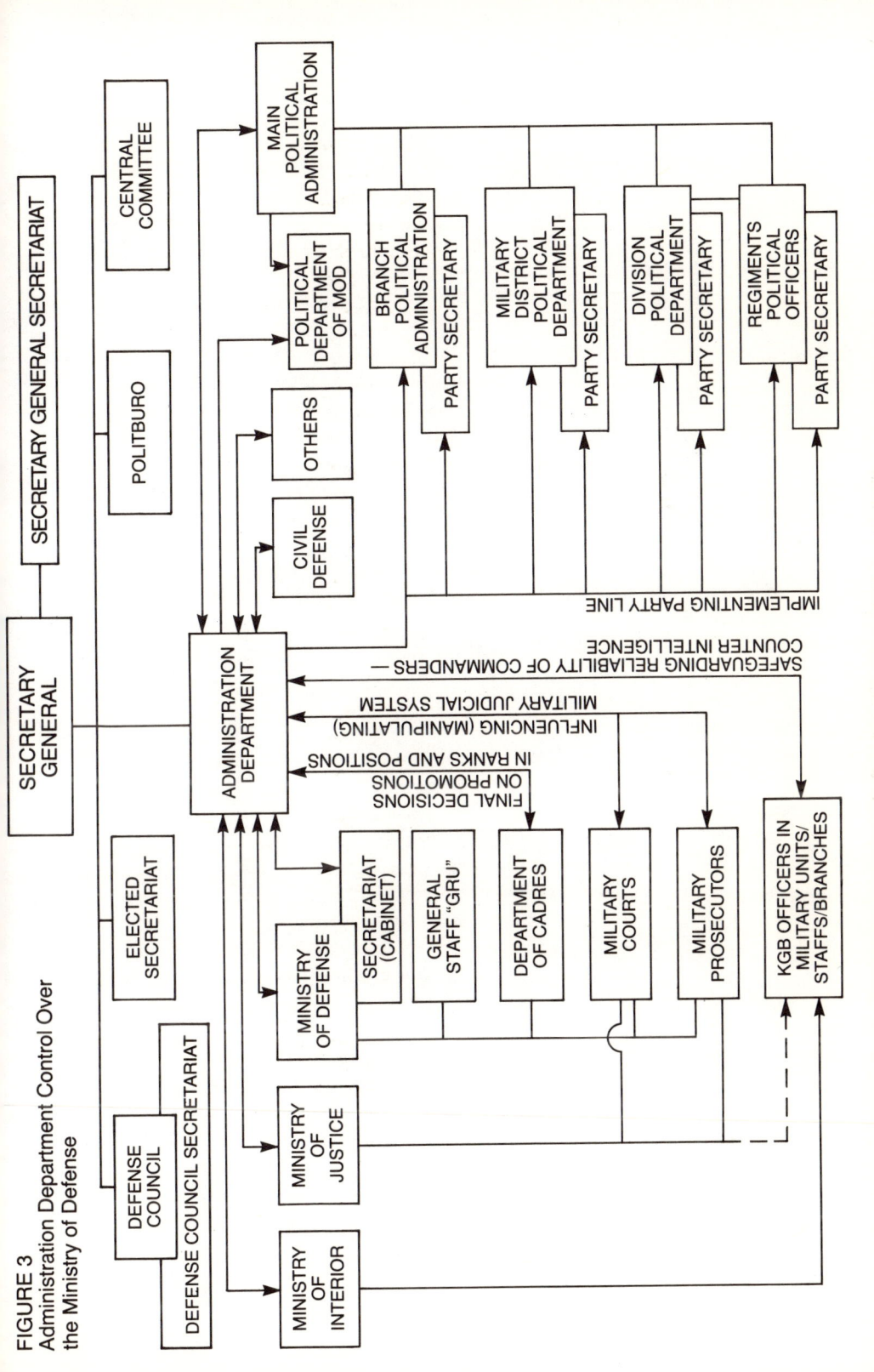

FIGURE 3
Administration Department Control Over the Ministry of Defense

line of work; they are not "elected," nor is there any pretense of election. Consequently, this group of bureaucrats is referred to as the non-elected Secretariat; they make up the Party apparatus. This secretariat is indicated by the gray area on Figure 1.

Similarly, there are secretariats at the republic, and regional (oblast in the Soviet Union) levels. These secretariats, in parallel fashion, are comprised of all the non-elected Party bureaucrats at the appropriate level. Here is where the power in the communist system is vested—i.e., in the totality of appointed Party bureaucrats. The people who wield that power are the secretaries and the heads of departments and sections.

The head of the non-elected Secretariat is the First Secretary or Secretary General. Under him are the individual secretaries who control the departments. These secretaries are "elected" as follows: the Party Organization Department recommends names to the Secretary General, who then sends his recommendations to the Central Committee for election. All secretaries by law are members of the Central Committee. Nomenklatura for them resides in the Central Committee; but, as indicated earlier, the recommendations are determined by the Elected Secretariat (the secretaries themselves) and announced by the Politburo. These "elected" secretaries, together with a few other selected officials, form the Elected Secretariat, which is chaired by the Secretary General.

From the decision-making point of view, the Elected Secretariat is one of the three key organizations referred to earlier. The principal members are all the secretaries of the Central Committee. The First Secretary, or Secretary General in the Soviet Union, is its Chairman. Other officials are invited on a regular basis to attend its weekly meetings. Of particular importance in this regard are the Chief of the Main Political Administration, the Chief Editor of *Pravda*, the heads of the Central Committee departments, and the chairmen of mass organizations (unions, women's and youth organizations). Meetings of the Secretariat are divided into two parts. At the first, all members participate. At the second session, all who are not secretaries are excluded. Among the most common items for discussion at the second session are personnel actions, i.e., hiring and firing, and deception.

The duty of the Elected Secretariat is to organize the day-to-day work of the Party machinery. The Secretariat discusses and makes decisions regarding internal Party concerns: for example, education of Party members; topics for discussion at various Party meetings; directives to the press, to cultural and propaganda agencies, and to mass organizations, regarding the Party "line"; and appointments of individuals to key positions in organizations in fields such as the press, foreign correspondents, scientific research, and cultural affairs. Thus, the Secretariat has nomenklatura over a considerable number of appointments.

Three areas of particular interest in which the Elected Secretariat functions are censorship and media; ideology, cultural affairs and the press; and deception. Ninety percent of the censorship decisions are controlled by the Secretariat. Each year it approves the list of classified information that is presented for approval by the ministers of Defense and Interior. There are four main classification levels: Office Use, Secret, Top Secret, and State Importance. Examples of the latter include plans of critical importance: operations, mobilization, evacuation, and intelligence. Examples of Top Secret items include directives for pursuing new technologies, making personnel changes, and participating in international negotiations. This classification also is often used to help control discussions bearing on future decisions; and, after the decision is made on a particular item, the classification may be downgraded. Each year the list of Secret and Top Secret items is prepared by the ministers of Interior and Defense.

In the military area, the Elected Secretariat is concerned with the direction of Party work (i.e., propaganda and culture) in the armed forces both in peace and in war. In matters of deception, the Secretariat performs important functions by ensuring that overt parts of deception operations, such as those concerning the press (both foreign and domestic), the diplomatic corps, scientific circles, and so forth, are carried out as directed by the Secretary General; and that strategic military deception operations are executed as directed by the Defense Council. In this regard, the Politburo, because of its nomenklatura functions, participates where personnel appointments are orchestrated as part of the deception.

The Politburo

The Politburo is one of the three most important Party organizations, the other two being the Defense Council and the Elected Secretariat. Of these three, *in reality*, the Politburo is the least important. It is composed mainly of the most important Party bureaucrats. The head of the Politburo is the Secretary General, who is assisted by the Deputy Secretary General. The other Politburo members are the first secretaries of the Central Committees of the most important republics and regions (that is, those who have broad responsibilities and areas of influence), together with the first secretaries of selected regions. In addition, there are usually about four members from the government, that is, from outside the Party bureaucratic apparatus. These are normally the Prime Minister, the Chairman of the State Planning Commission, the Minister of Defense, and occasionally the Interior or Foreign Minister. As can be seen, the secretaries control the Politburo, which helps explain why in practice the Elected Secretariat is more important than the Politburo.

The Politburo is concerned with day-to-day policy actions of the Party, and most of these, perhaps 75 percent, are concerned with economic and social issues. Its principal focus of attention is the short-term plan, and, in particular, it tends to review one-year plans each quarter and one-month plans each month. The Politburo also deals with general Party policy and, to a limited extent, with foreign policy. The Politburo also approves all new laws before they are submitted to the National Assembly—or, in the Soviet Union, to the Supreme Soviet. The Politburo is not empowered to discuss top secret defense and intelligence matters.

The Politburo meets once a week, usually in the afternoon. The Chairman of the Politburo, the Secretary General, has his own Secretariat, which draws up the plans and agenda for Politburo meetings. Following each meeting, the Secretariat prepares the minutes of the meeting and delivers the decisions of the Politburo to the officials responsible for implementing them.

The Politburo in theory has nomenklatura over generals and marshals in the Soviet Union and over all key positions such as the Chief of the General Staff, the commands of the military districts, the deputy ministers, and the ambassadors. However, this power is in reality a rubber-stamp operation, because it is the recommendations of the Party apparatus that the Politburo is approving, with each department being responsible for the recommendations to fill the key positions in its area of authority. For example, appointments for the Chief of the General Staff and the commands of the military districts are recommended by the Administration Department; ambassadors are recommended by the Foreign Department (in the Soviet Union by the International Department and the Foreign Cadres Department). Moreover, the departments control the information supporting their recommendations, and Politburo members as a general rule do not have independent means of ascertaining the accuracy of this information.

3.
Government and National Assembly

IN THE COMMUNIST system, all power resides in the Party. At the same time, there is a major effort to provide an image of democratic respectability, to project the image of a government that represents the people, one that is even more "democratic" than the U.S. political system. Projecting this image is the primary function of the government, the parliament (the National Assembly in Czechoslovakia, the Supreme Soviet in the Soviet Union), and the Constitution. They are all a deception oriented toward the West and the Third World. They show the Soviet Union, in particular, as a socialist democracy in which the people have the same rights guaranteed through the Constitution as do the people in the United States. By covering the totalitarian system with the trappings of democracy, the Soviet Union invests itself with the respectability of democracy, and at the same time real democracies are implicitly degraded by association.

The National Assembly is the body of "elected" representatives, and the government or Council of Ministers is the collection of appointed executives that oversee the ministries and other government bodies. The National Assembly is mainly responsible for the Constitution and changes thereto, international treaties, new laws, and control of the government. These responsibilities are only de jure, however, because laws and treaties are first formulated and approved by the Party before they go to the Assembly, and because the Assembly has too little knowledge about government activities and resources to be able in any sense of the word to control or supervise government operations; it can only criticize the government for failure to follow the Party line, or at least couch criticisms in that context.

The National Assembly is "elected" in theory. In practice, however, its members are approved by the Central Committee, which has nomenklatura over the positions, based on the recommendations of Central Committee departments and secretaries. The same is true for government executives. Again, true power resides, ultimately, in the Party, more specifically in the Secretary General, the Central Committee secretaries, and the departments.

Neither the parliament nor the government has effective power. The National Assembly meets only a few times each year; the government, once a month. Within the parliament and government, what little power there is is wielded by their respective presidiums. Sejna was a member of the National Assembly from 1954 to 1968 and a member of its Presidium from

1964 to 1968. These presidiums have the same rights as the government and the parliament and act on their behalf. When an action or "decision" is attributed to government or parliament, it is most likely an action of the respective presidium. For example, in the Polish Constitution, declaration of martial law is the responsibility of the National Assembly. But the Assembly was not called until several weeks after martial law was declared in December 1981—the Presidium had approved the declaration. In the case of personnel matters, the National Assembly presumably reviews and approves all ministerial actions. However, when Barak, the Czechoslovak Minister of Interior, was fired, he was in jail for two weeks before the issue was presented to the Presidium of the National Assembly (it was never presented to the Assembly itself).

The government Presidium is composed of the Prime Minister and several deputy prime ministers, who in a sense are government counterparts of the Central Committee secretaries. The Presidium is somewhat analogous to the Politburo. Each deputy has the responsibility for coordinating the activities of the ministries and other government bodies under his supervision. It is important to understand that two ministries, Defense and Interior (StB), *do not report to the government*; they report only to the Administration Department and directly to the Secretary General. The National Assembly Presidium is headed by a chairman, who is often the Secretary General. In his capacity as chairman, he is referred to as the "Collective President."

The difference between the Prime Minister and the Secretary General can be appreciated in Khrushchev's guidance to Czechoslovakia's Secretary General Novotny following the Soviet leader's meeting with President Kennedy in June 1961. On his way back to Moscow, Khrushchev briefed Novotny on the outcome of the summit. Novotny subsequently summarized Khrushchev's conclusions for the Defense Council. Khrushchev had said that Kennedy was an intelligent man with whom it would be possible to work out an accommodation within the framework of peaceful coexistence. But Kennedy had said that Khrushchev should understand that it was impossible overnight to change U.S. perceptions of the USSR; he had won the presidential election only by a narrow margin and there were powerful constituencies in his country that were opposed to a more flexible attitude toward the Soviet Union.

Khrushchev's main conclusion was that the bloc should take an understanding view toward Kennedy's predicament but should keep up steady pressure on his Administration to maintain the pace of accommodation. But the bloc should be discrete in its attacks and should focus them on the opponents of peaceful coexistence; it was necessary to divide the West, not unite it by crude attacks on capitalism. That was not to say that Khrushchev was prepared to restrain the international communist movement. Quite the contrary, he told Novotny. It must be made clear to all communists that he had spoken to Kennedy as Chairman of the Council of Ministers of the Soviet Union. But as Secretary General of the Soviet Communist Party, and leader of the world communist movement, his hands were free; indeed, one of the main objectives of peaceful coexistence was to improve the climate for the spread of communism.

Nothing goes to the government for discussion or decision without first having been passed on by some Party body. And then, consideration by the government is only pro forma. For example, in the Czechoslovak Constitution, the Defense Council is given authority to declare war. This declaration is then subject to the approval of the National Assembly—but, to what use, if the war has already been started! The department of the Central Committee that is in charge of activities of the government and parliament is the Department of Elected State Organs, which in satellite countries is normally under the Secretary in charge of ideology. In the Soviet Union, it is usually under the Deputy Secretary General.

Besides the ministries of Defense and Interior, the most important ministries are the Foreign Ministry, which is the government counterpart of the Party's International Department; the Ministry for Foreign Trade; the Ministry of Science (Committee of Science in the Soviet Union); and, in the Soviet Union, the Ministry of Military Production.

Throughout the government and parliament, control is exercised by the leaders of "Party groups" in much the same way that control at the Party Congress is exercised through delegation heads. Within each governmental and mass organization, such as ministries and unions, the members who belong to the Communist Party form what is called a Party group. The leader of each Party group is appointed by the Elected Secretariat and is always one of the top Party leaders. The leader of the Party group in the National Assembly and the government is a secretary of the Central Committee. When there are issues to discuss or directions to be given, these leaders assemble their groups and impart to them the wisdom of the Politburo, including how they are to vote on all issues and elections.

A good example of how the Party group operates took place in early 1967, just before Sejna defected, when the Minister of Interior presented to the National Assembly a new law governing the secret police. A member of the Assembly who was also a member of the Central Committee stood up and asked if, under the new law, the secret police could arrest the President or Secretary General whenever they wanted and keep him in jail. The Minister replied that this could happen if the Secretary General or President did not have the proper papers on his person to identify him as the Secretary General or President. The majority voted against the law—the first time such an action had been taken, and a reflection of the turbulent times in Czechoslovakia in late 1967 and early 1968, when an ouster of

Novotny was being orchestrated in favor of Dubcek. Before the members of the Party group had reached home following the meeting of parliament and the unprecedented vote, telegrams had been delivered to their homes calling a meeting of the Party group at 9:00 a.m. the following day. At that meeting, the Deputy Secretary General presented a stern lecture on Party unity and discipline. A half-hour later a meeting of the National Assembly was called and a second vote was taken. This time it passed unanimously. That is how the system works.

The principal issues that the government and parliament address are economic issues. In the case of military and security matters, only simple items are discussed or "decided": for example, new laws dealing with the draft; the promotion of generals and marshals, which are first approved by the Politburo after being recommended by the Administration Department; statutes of military schools; the nomination of professors at military schools; and the open (i.e., non-secret) part of the military budget.

The ministers, such as the Foreign Minister and Minister of Defense, are the government officials "responsible" under the Constitution to the government for their respective ministries. They are also, in general, members of the National Assembly and, more important, members of the Central Committee. While they may be "responsible" to the government, in reality they are held responsible by the Party, specifically by the departments that have cognizance over the particular ministries. The department secretaries are, therefore, far stronger than the minister.

Within each department, specific sections normally are responsible for the ministries. For example, within the Administration Department, there are sections that correspond to the Ministry of Defense, the Ministry of Justice, the Ministry of Interior, and the Military Organization (Svazarm in Czechoslovakia, DOSAF in the Soviet Union). The Ministry of Interior is actually the Czechoslovak equivalent of the Soviet KGB. Thus, the term Interior is used in the sense of internal security and as such should not be confused with the use of "Interior" in Western governments. In practice, the ministers report to the heads of these sections; and, as indicated earlier, these heads are more powerful and more knowledgeable than the ministers.

The minister really has little power. He only has the duty to carry out the decisions that he may receive from any one of five sources: the Secretary General, the Elected Secretariat, the Defense Council, the Politburo, and a Central Committee secretary. For example, perhaps the most important plan is the five-year plan. The ministers who are expected to carry out the detailed plans in their respective areas, if they are fortunate, may have the opportunity to help prepare the plans. Whether or not they do, these ministers have the task of actually presenting the detailed plans to the Politburo or Defense Council for approval. These detailed plans outline what the minister will do to implement the political directives that are to be approved at the Party Congress. While the ministers are responsible for and control their ministries, it is the department heads who control the implementation of the plans. But it is the minister who is responsible for carrying out the plan. That is, the Party has no responsibility. The Party does not make mistakes. If something is wrong with the plan, it is the minister's fault, not the Party's. Thus, we see another aspect of government deception. While decisions are made by the Party, responsibility for failure is placed on the ministers, and in this manner, on the government. The Party is responsible only for success; the government is the scapegoat for failure.

4.
Military Decision-Making

The Defense Council

THE DEFENSE COUNCIL is the highest level decision-making body in Soviet communist systems with responsibility for intelligence, counter-intelligence, military affairs, foreign policy, economics, and industry. Its responsibility and authority flow mainly from its primary mission, which is to protect socialism and its global domination objective. Anything that can affect the progress of socialism, either at home or abroad, is the province of the Defense Council. The more specific tasks within its purview include the defense of the country, readiness of the military forces, information on the enemy (intelligence and counter-intelligence operations), international collective defense, subversive and terrorist activities, strategic deception, political and military strategy, and associated plans and preparations for the conduct of war.

As indicated earlier, the Politburo deals chiefly with internal financial, economic, social, and Party matters. In contrast, the Defense Council is concerned with the political and military strategy of the State.

While the Politburo would discuss open treaties with foreign countries, it is only in the Defense Council that political strategy, intelligence, and military operations in foreign countries are examined. The Politburo would not be privy to those discussions except as recommended by the Defense Council and approved by the Secretary General. Similarly, the Politburo may discuss a resolution, for example, against American "aggression" in Nicaragua, to be presented at the United Nations, because such a resolution is propaganda and not secret. However, if the issue is whether to send more weapons to Nicaragua, that item would be considered by the Defense Council, not by the Politburo.

The Secretary General is automatically the Chairman of the Defense Council; his deputy is also the Council's Deputy Chairman. Its other members are the Prime Minister, the Minister of Interior, the Chief of the State Planning Commission, and the Minister of Defense. These positions are set forth in law and the appointments are all approved by the Politburo. While all the members may also be members of the Politburo, this is not necessary.

Coordination, administration, and staff work in support of the Defense Council is orchestrated by its Secretary, who heads the Council's Secretariat. The Secretary is normally the Chief of the General Staff and the Secretariat is usually an element of the General Staff. This practice is part of what is referred to as an "integrated" defense system (that is, a defense system, in both military and civilian aspects, that is in place during peacetime and organized so as to minimize disruption and delay when war begins.) As is frequently the case, however, there are exceptions, and Czechoslovakia in the late 1950s and 1960s provides a good example of such an exception.

In Czechoslovakia, the Defense Council was formed in June 1956, although at that time it was called the Military Committee of the Central Committee. It did not adopt the name Defense Council, or, more formally, the Highest Council of the Defense of the Country, until 1969. Prior to 1956, the *Trojka* (composed of the First Secretary, Minister of Defense, and Chief of Secret Police) performed the role of Defense Council under the direction of the Soviet Union, where all of the key defense decisions were made. Part of Khrushchev's modernization program in the mid-1950s was to recall most of the Soviet advisers from Czechoslovakia and instruct the Czechoslovaks to organize their own Defense Council, subject, of course, to Soviet oversight and approval.

When the Defense Council was first formed, the Chief of the General Staff was not on it, nor was the Secretariat housed in the General Staff area. The exclusion of the Chief of the General Staff was due to Soviet distrust of his bourgeois background. In his place, Sejna, as the ranking political officer and Chief of Staff of the Minister of Defense, was appointed head of the Defense Council Secretariat. Acting in this capacity, roughly in July 1956, Sejna prepared the Czech statutes regarding the responsibilities and organization of the Czechoslovak military organizations.

These Czechoslovak military organizations (the Defense Council, General Staff, Ministry of Defense) were modeled after their Soviet counterparts. For this purpose, Sejna had access to top secret Soviet statutes and regulations governing the Soviet Defense Council and related organizations. Thus, the Defense Council became a copy of the Soviet Defense Council, with similar responsibilities, procedures, and structures, albeit on a smaller satellite scale. Even Defense Council membership, as previously set forth, was identical to that of its Soviet counterpart. This membership was deliberately kept small by the Soviets to guard against undesired dissemination of information. The similarity between Soviet and satellite country organizations and practices permeates all levels and areas of Party and government operations. Officials such as Sejna traveled to the Soviet Union several times each year to ensure they did things correctly, i.e., that their operations were based on the Soviet model, to "take advantage" of the many years of Soviet experience and evolution.

The Czechoslovak Defense Council met every other week on Wednesday afternoon. The agenda for the meeting was prepared in advance and all decisions were carefully coordinated, i.e., reached before the meeting. The meetings were held principally to render formal decisions. Discussion was minimal except in the case of emergency items on the agenda, which may not have been fully coordinated in advance. Even information items that were presented mainly to advise the members of important developments led to decisions, such as to continue an action previously adopted.

Defense Council agenda items for decision consisted of regularly scheduled, non-regularly scheduled, and emergency matters. The most important *regularly scheduled* decision items included:

- March: Review and approval of the Operation Plan for the coming year.
- May: Biannual review and approval of the plan for development of military technology and acquisition of modern weapons systems.
- June: Mid-year review of progress in implementing the intelligence plan.
- June: Mid-year review of the technical espionage plan.
- October: Biannual review and approval of the plan for development of military technology and acquisition of modern weapons systems.
- October-November: Review and approval of the armed forces' training program and schedule for the coming year.
- October-November: Review and approval of the special budget, which is the secret part of the budget.
- November: Review of technical espionage activity (both civilian and military).
- November: Review of the technical espionage plan for the next year.
- December: Review and approval of the intelligence plan.
- December: Review and approval of the material and supply plan.
- December: Review and approval of the mobilization plan for the coming year.

Probably the most important example of the Defense Council decision process is that associated with the Operation Plan. This is the most important plan because it has a major impact on all vital aspects of Czechoslovak society—the economy, finance, agriculture, construction, industry, intelligence, and the military. The Operation Plan is unusual in that no documentation regarding it is ever delivered to the Defense Council. When the time comes for the Defense Council to review the Operation Plan and approve it, the Council goes to the General Staff—in particular, to the Operations Administration within the General Staff. There, the Chief of the

General Staff and the Head of the Operations Administration explain the tasks assigned to the armed forces, how they are to be carried out, what capabilities are needed to carry out those tasks, and with what other satellite forces (on the left and right flanks) to cooperate. To a considerable degree, these "tasks" constitute the Soviet input to each of the Warsaw Pact countries at the start of the planning cycle and are designed to ensure that the various country plans are coordinated with, or more accurately are a part of, Soviet plans. The final review of the completed plans by the Defense Council is a very complicated and intense process, taking one or two days. After the Operation Plan is approved by the Defense Council, the Soviet Supreme Commander of all Warsaw Pact armed forces visits each country. His signature is the final approval; without it, the plan is meaningless. This is another important example of how the Soviet Union controls the satellite countries.

The material and technical supply plan is developed as part of the Operation Plan but is considered separately. The approval process for this plan is more complicated now than in the past because today decisions must pass first through the Comecon, which is designed to coordinate technology development among Warsaw Pact members. This is done to ensure that each country contributes in areas in which it has a comparative advantage, in the interest of efficiency. All Comecon departments contain military sections, which have representatives from the Pact nations and which coordinate all aspects of development, procurement, and, where appropriate, military assistance. After the Comecon coordinates the organization of technology development among the member nations, the Czechoslovak material and technical supply plan is submitted to the Czechoslovak Defense Council for final approval.

In the case of the development of military technology, there are one-year plans that are reviewed twice a year, and there are longer-range plans. A week before a decision on the plan involving procurement of weapons and equipment is to be made, documents appraising technological developments are sent to the Defense Council. These documents summarize the positive and negative features of the weapons and equipment, their status in the testing cycle, estimated production costs, and such things as the volume of the expected production run and its disposition—that is, how much of it will go to supply Warsaw Pact forces, how much to overseas military sales, and how much to national forces. In the case of sensitive technology—for example, the acquisition of new air defense sites—the documents also provide details on the organization of deception which will serve to hide the activity.

Immediately before the final decision on weapons and equipment is reached, the Ministry of Defense organizes a show for the Defense Council at a convenient military base to demonstrate to Council members all the items on which they must reach a decision. This is generally a one-day show. On the following day, a case-by-case review of the recommendations of the Minister of Defense is conducted by the Defense Council. At that point decisions are made on how many of which items are to be produced and to which countries the items will be sold or transferred. From there, the decisions go to the appropriate ministries for implementation.

The most important *non-regularly scheduled* items for discussion and approval by the Defense Council include large-scale military maneuvers, the evacuation plan, training foreign students, weapons trade and supply to non-Warsaw Pact countries, and civil defense, as well as other items that occur less frequently, such as the five-year plan and long-range plan. Below are additional examples of non-regularly scheduled items for decision, which indicate the breadth of Defense Council interests and responsibilities:

- Infiltration and manipulation of the foreign media.
- Exploitation of Third World countries (for example, to use their votes against the United States in international forums, to establish military bases, etc.).
- Exploitation of religions, especially Catholicism (for example, to use Latin American priests to support the communist cause).
- Infiltration and exploitation of financial and economic institutions for the revolutionary process.
- Bloc aid and activities to strengthen communist movements in Latin America.
- Exploitation of political differences between the "power circles" and minorities in the West.
- Participation of the Czechoslovak Party as part of Soviet operations: for example, to mobilize the Western media in support of Lyndon Johnson in the 1964 presidential election.
- Czechoslovakia's role in support of isolationist tendencies in the United States.
- Review of a special report on the "Green International," that is, the Social Democratic movement.
- Review of reports on Third World countries (Ghana, Mali, Algeria, Egypt, Syria, Ethiopia, Mexico, Dominican Republic, and Argentina) where the Czechoslovaks had special responsibilities.
- Review of special reports on developments in Poland and on the activities of Czechoslovak diplomatic and intelligence efforts in Poland, in the wake of the Hungarian revolution.
- Review of a report on the plan for transition from a peace economy to a war economy, under which mobilization time was cut from six months to three months. As part of the change, special units were established at each institute, office, factory, etc., to organize the transition.

- Review of developments in Vietnam during the war. Many sessions—three or four a year—were held on this subject, dealing with the supply of military materials to North Vietnam, the course of the war and the role of the United States, and, of special importance, the exploitation of the worldwide media against the United States.
- Review of the role of the communist and noncommunist media in promoting communist objectives. This was a subject for special discussion at least six times from 1956 to 1958, and scientific and cultural institutions and leading individuals in these fields were the subject of at least three discussions.
- Review of reports on the collapse of communist movements in Ghana and Indonesia. These reports were very critical of intelligence and counter-intelligence activities in the subject countries.

A good example of non-regularly scheduled action by the Defense Council is the development of evacuation plans, which were first spelled out in the five-year plan of 1960 and afterward appeared in one-year plans. After the decision to develop evacuation plans was taken, responsibility for implementation of the decision was passed from the Secretary of the Defense Council to the appropriate ministers—Health, Defense, Interior, Transportation, and Communications—and to the defense councils of the various regions. In this case, the principal responsibility for overseeing the process was assigned to the Minister of Health, and it was his responsibility to report back to the Defense Council on the progress of evacuation plans.

At the same time, major control over the development of evacuation plans—overseeing activities in all responsible ministries—was assigned to the Administration Department. Each ministry prepared appropriate guidelines and rules for evacuation that were to be submitted to the Politburo for approval. At the same time, each ministry began work on detailed implementation plans for evacuation. Wherever problems arose, the Administration Department would resolve them—if necessary, the decision would be made by the Secretary General. The underlying philosophy in this case, and in others, is that one should not take problems to the Defense Council; they are to be resolved before the issue is presented to the Council for decision.

In the case of regularly and non-regularly scheduled items, all pertinent documents are to be delivered, by law, to Council members one week prior to the meeting at which decisions based on the documents are made. Exceptions to this rule are the intelligence and operation plans, which are not reviewed in advance by the Council membership as a whole. Decisions are well prepared and the decision-making session tends to be pro forma in nature—another example of the principle of Party unity in action. At the meetings, everyone agrees; there is no dissension. The key figures in preparing the agenda are the Secretary of the Defense Council and the head of the Administration Department, with the Secretary General making the final decisions.

For each item on the agenda, the Secretary General assigns to an appropriate individual—for example, the chief Party bureaucrat or responsible member of the Defense Council—the task of coordinating the decision process in advance, ensuring that all problems are resolved and implementation plans are prepared in advance. Thus, when a decision is "finally reached" at a meeting, its implementation plans, control, oversight, and secrecy measures have all been worked out in advance and are approved as part of the "decision." Each agency affected by the decision participates by working out its portion of the implementing plan. The paper work is prepared by the Defense Council Secretariat, which performs mainly an administrative function. Where Party strategy or major intelligence or defense issues are involved, this work is done by appropriate sections of the Administration Department, for example, the interior and military sections. Where money is involved, preparation work is performed by the Military Administration in the State Planning Commission and in the Finance Ministry. These military administrations and section chiefs at the Administration Department often wield the real power in the decision process. The military administrations also play the key role in developing the secret part of the budget that is approved by the Defense Council and is not sent to the Politburo. Incidentally, there are also secret parts of the one-year and five-year plans that are not submitted to the Politburo or to the parliament.

The third type of decision items scheduled at the discretion of the Secretary General are designated *emergency*. By their very nature, paperwork cannot be completed in advance, nor is there time to coordinate the decisions. Consequently, on these items there is discussion and debate to the extent permitted by the Secretary General. Because the items are not prepared in advance and documents are not passed to the membership, non-regularly scheduled items that are very sensitive and subject to tight secrecy are also treated as emergency items. One especially important example of this latter use of the "emergency" classification is the weapons system acquisition plan. While this plan is really part of the Operation Plan, it is treated as a separate "emergency decision" to restrict its dissemination until the final decision is made. Other examples of emergency items on the Czechoslovak Defense Council agenda in the late 1950s are:

- Review of intelligence service and secret Party operations to force the "imperialists" to accept the peaceful coexistence policy. (1956)
- The use of Czechoslovak influence (organizations, people, etc.) in foreign countries in support of peaceful coexistence. (1957)
- Efforts to wage political and psychological warfare in Europe, especially plans for propaganda and deception associated with the possible outbreak of war in Central Europe. (1958)
- Review of reports prepared both before and after the 21st Party Congress on how to exploit Czechoslovak industry to improve military technology for Warsaw Pact forces—a program associated with the Brezhnev long-range planning effort and its implementation.
- The supply of money, training, and military equipment and weapons to terrorist movements. This subject was discussed twice a year from at least as early as 1956 through 1968, and sometimes three or four times a year. At the time these movements were active in Angola and Mozambique, it was discussed practically every month. While terrorist activities in general were continuous, there were decisions on two occasions to intensify terrorist operations: one in 1958, after the 20th Party Congress, and again after the Khrushchev/Kennedy meeting in Vienna in 1961. The latter step-up in revolutionary activities followed the agreement that Kennedy and Khrushchev reached, to the effect that terrorism was a local problem, the result of poor management or poor distribution of resources locally, and was not a communist-instigated problem. The countries of special interest in the terrorist movement from the Czechoslovak point of view were Angola, Mozambique, Algeria, all of Latin America, Cyprus, Turkey, Rhodesia, Northern Ireland, and South Africa.
- The supply and training of military forces from Third World countries. This was a subject for discussion and decision at least twice a year, and included, at various times, key states such as Egypt, Syria, Iraq, Ghana, Cambodia, Mali, Guiana, Cuba, Vietnam, India, and Indonesia. It is important in considering the training of Third World personnel to recognize that there were two groups of such people: one was known to the leaders of individual Third World nations, and the second group was secret, unknown to the government of the nation from which the trainees came.

In the 1960s there were many emergency items connected with the buildup of military capabilities within the Warsaw Pact:

- 1960-1961: Decision on the principles for selection of special elites in Western countries for recruitment to the communist cause.
- 1961-1962: Emergency report on the progress of the effort to select special elites.
- 1961: Emergency plans for the production and deployment of anti-aircraft missiles.
- 1963: Decision on the sabotage plan and on separate actions to supply materials for sabotage groups. These plans were generally examined every six months and reviewed in discussions of the intelligence plans. The Czechoslovaks played a key role in the plan for the United Kingdom, France, Germany, Austria, Switzerland, Belgium, Norway, Canada, and the Middle East.
- 1963: Emergency discussion of the assassination of President Kennedy and assessment of its meaning for peaceful coexistence, deception and intelligence plans, and NATO influence operations.
- 1963: Emergency decisions on reserve railroads and highways to bypass cities or provide parallel routes from the Soviet Union to the central front. Emergency meetings on this topic were also held in 1964 and 1967.
- 1964: Emergency decisions on the building of a radio-technical center and support facilities for intelligence operations.
- 1964: Emergency decisions on special nuclear, biological, and chemical (NBC) weapons warehouses and reserves for Soviet troops. This was repeated in 1966.
- 1964: Emergency decisions on plans related to artillery missiles (their acquisition, storage, cost, and training of troops).
- November 1964: Emergency sessions were held after the intelligence meeting in Moscow to discuss procurement of advanced technology for the intelligence service, the strengthening of sabotage and diversion units, and the unification of the information system whereby intelligence would flow first to Moscow and then back to the respective nations.
- 1965-1966: Emergency decisions on the security plan for transporting nuclear warheads.
- 1966: Emergency decisions to buy and deploy the first three Su-7s for nuclear delivery.

The above emergency decisions were all associated with operations of special sensitivity. Crisis situations involving emergency discussions included the Hungarian Revolution (1956), the Congo crisis (Lumumba's assassination in 1960), the Berlin crisis (1961), the Cuban crisis (1962), the Middle East war (1967), and the Vietnam war (when the U.S. government in 1967 issued a statement on the possibility of blockading Haiphong harbor). Emergency sessions were also held to discuss the infiltration of Poland by Czechoslovak agents when Gomulka took power, and also the infiltration of China, Yugoslavia, and Rumania by Czechoslovak agents.

In the crisis situations identified above—the Hungarian revolution, the Berlin crisis, and the Cuban crisis—there was direct connection between the Defense Councils in the Warsaw Pact countries and the Defense Council in the Soviet Union. In these crises, it was possible to observe the Soviet system in operation, especially the dominant role of the Defense Council (not the Politburo) in making decisions and directing action. Decisions were constantly arriving in Prague, indicating that the Soviet Defense Council was operating in almost continuous session, as were the Defense Councils of the other Warsaw Pact countries. In these cases, the principal action taken was mobilization—both to communicate to the West that the Warsaw Pact countries were ready for war, in a posture to intimidate the West; and also to ensure that the Warsaw Pact countries were prepared for war, in the sense of not trusting the West.

These cases illustrate how the Defense Council would operate in the event of war. The regular meetings of many bodies, for example, the Ministry of Defense Kolegium and the Main Military Council, would be discontinued since the officials who would normally take part in those meetings would be commanding forces in the field. The Defense Council itself would be in almost permanent session and would be co-located with the General Staff. Various key individuals, such as the Chief of the General Staff, the Chief of the GRU, and the Chief of Civilian Intelligence, would keep the Defense Council informed within their areas of expertise and would recommend decisions. In a crisis situation, there would not be much supporting paperwork. The process would be one of operations, operational decisions, and getting decisions to the people to implement them. Paperwork and advance coordination would be dispensed with. The chiefs of the various organizations, such as those identified above, would receive decisions on the spot and immediately transmit those decisions to the proper individuals, sometimes even ordering the latter to come immediately to the meeting so they could communicate the decisions verbally. Timing is extremely important in such situations.

In the present era, crises can arise rapidly. The time factor is especially critical in a nuclear crisis because of the danger of surprise attack and the need to respond instantly to critical information. The Soviets place major emphasis on having wartime organizations constituted and operating in peacetime—another aspect of "integrating" the defense system. Officials who will be making the critical decisions have to be trained in peacetime to be familiar with all aspects of the war plans.

In crises or war, the Defense Council goes into emergency permanent session and becomes the Supreme Command. Its actual composition is not set forth in the law and is, therefore, subject to the decision of the supreme commander, who is the Secretary General and head of the Defense Council. There is considerable confusion in the West concerning the supreme command, that is, where responsibility lies for crisis management and the conduct of war. This responsibility lies with the Defense Council, which would take decisions with the advice and support of the key individuals whose task it would be to carry out the decisions. The meeting body will vary in size: the Defense Council, the core, is augmented from time to time as its members desire by the most important advisers (for example, the Commander of Warsaw Pact Forces; Commander-in-Chief of the Strategic Rocket Forces; head of the International Department; head of the General Staff Operations Administration; head of appropriate military districts, and so forth). This speeds the decision and implementation process, and it ensures proper consideration of details, as well as an understanding and clear acceptance of responsibility by those charged with carrying out the decisions.

Should war be imminent, the Defense Council would be the first to move to the underground command bunkers along with the operations section of the Operations Administration and representatives of all elements of the Ministry of Defense. The deputies of these organizations and elements would be relocated to a reserve command post. Duplicate sets of plans are prepared and prepositioned at safeguarded strategic locations; other duplicates are kept ready for evacuation to the underground and reserve command posts. To further ensure continuity of command through the crucial initial period of a war, major commands would have some form of alternate command responsibility.

The Ministry of Defense

The Ministry of Defense (MOD), in the organizational structure, is under the Administration Department, along with Justice, DOSAF, and Interior. The main organizations under the MOD are shown in Figure 4. With regard to military operations and plans, the Minister of Defense reports to and takes direction from the Defense Council. Within the Ministry the principal organizations, insofar as we are concerned here, are the Secretariat, the Main Party Committee, the Kolegium, the Main Military Council, the General Staff, the military districts, and the various services.

Secretariat. The Secretariat (sometimes referred to as the Cabinet) of the Minister of Defense is responsible for the flow of paper to and from

FIGURE 4
Czechoslovak Ministry of Defense and General Staff Agencies

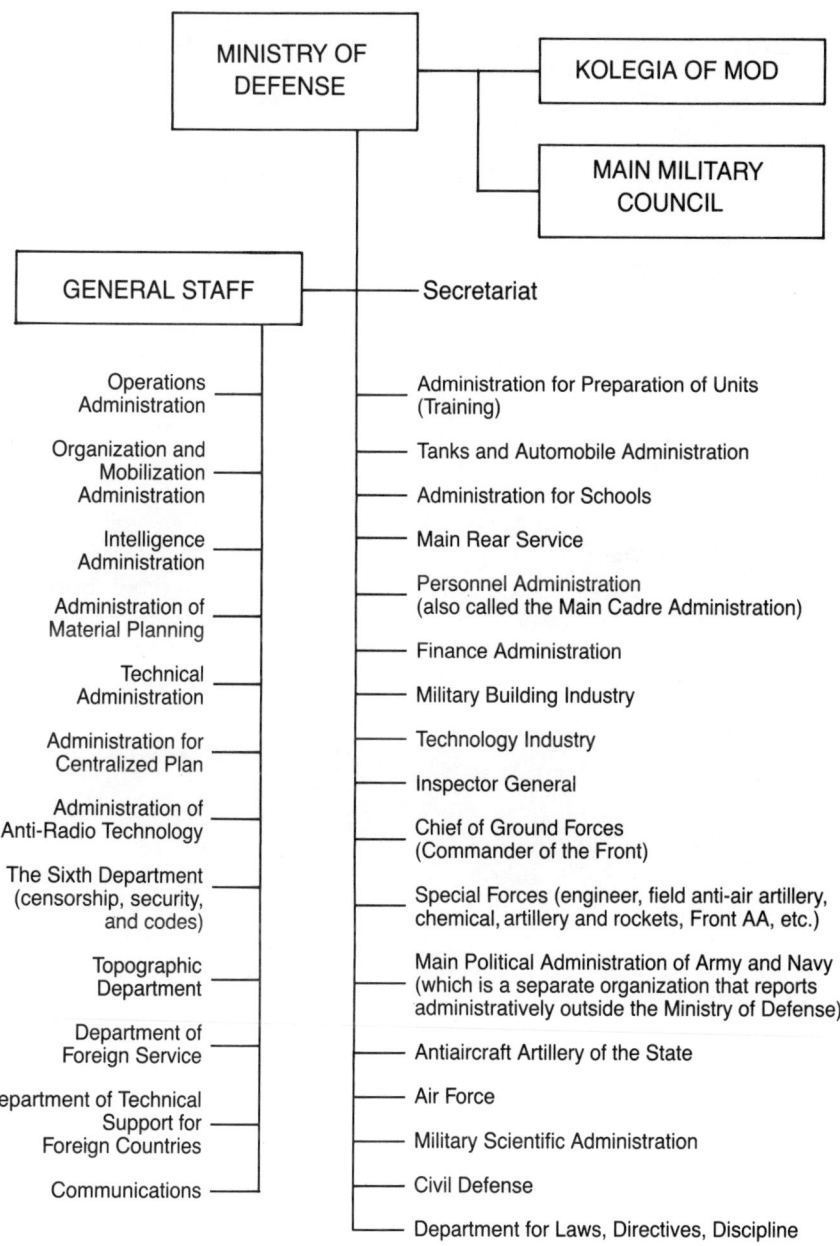

the Minister. In 1956, Sejna was appointed Chief of the Secretariat by Novotny, who at that time was First Secretary. Sejna's job was to ensure that all decisions were in accordance with Party policy.

All recommendations from the Minister of Defense to the Politburo, to the Soviet General Staff, and to the Defense Council passed through Sejna's hands and had to be examined in light of Soviet directives and Party guidelines. He was also responsible for scrutinizing all instructions from the Party and from Soviet leaders to the Minister and for providing the Minister with a list of recommendations on ways to implement these directives. His Secretariat was composed of five departments, all headed by Sejna. (1) The Special Department was the most secret; it controlled all correspondence between the Minister, the Red Army, and the highest organs of the Party, including all strategic plans (the General Staff held the operation and mobilization plans). This department also held the archives of the Defense Council. (2) The Legislative Department was responsible for protecting the legal interests of the armed forces from any encroachments likely to arise from intended legislation or policy. (3) The Inspection Department had the duty of inquiring into any aspect of military discipline and capability meriting its concern. (4) The Legal Department defended the Ministry in court and dealt with letters from the public to the Minister. (5) The Organization Department was in charge of the Minister's entertaining and hospitality; it ran VIP villas for the use of visiting Soviet officials and made these available to other ministries (especially the Interior Ministry and Central Committee), when appropriate. It was also responsible for communicating the Minister's orders to the Army.

Main Party Committee. This organization is directly under the Central Committee. The First Secretary of the Main Party Committee is automatically a member of the military section of the Administration Department, the Kolegium of the Ministry of Defense, and the Bureau of the Main Political Administration. Sejna was appointed First Secretary in 1964. In this capacity, he was responsible to the Central Committee for directing Party work at the Ministry of Defense. To assist him in this activity, he had a Party Committee, and his own bureau, secretariat, and control and discipline committee. As First Secretary, he was responsible for ensuring that decisions of higher Party bodies—Secretary General, Central Committee, Politburo, Defense Council, Elected Secretariat— were correctly implemented within the Ministry of Defense. Among other things, he ensured that the cadres (i.e., personnel) policy promulgated by the Central Committee was implemented; operated his own nomenklatura over all officers below the level of colonel (colonel and above come under the nomenklatura of the Administration Department and Politburo); and was in charge of security at the Ministry of Defense, of ideology and propaganda, and of unions and youth movements. Finally, it was his responsibility to make sure that mobilization and readiness at the Ministry of Defense was maintained at the proper level.

Kolegium. The Kolegium is a small group (ten in Czechoslovakia, fifteen in the Soviet Union) of senior officials who act almost as a "preliminary" Defense Council at the Ministry of Defense. Kolegia exist in all ministries, and members are usually appointed by the Politburo. The exceptions are the kolegia at the ministries of Defense and Interior, which are appointed by the Defense Council.

At the Ministry of Defense, the Kolegium is run by the Minister. Defense issues that ultimately are to go to the Defense Council, except the operation and intelligence plans, go first to the Kolegium for review and recommendation. Decisions are often made on issues or programs by the Minister at meetings of the Kolegium, which functions as both a defense review and oversight arm of the Defense Council.

The Kolegium is one body where unity is not the rule—specifically because it is a Party body, exercising oversight within a ministry, and designed to bring exceptions or disagreements with internal ministry decisions to the attention of the Party. Each member of the Kolegium has the right *and duty* to call on the Chairman of the Defense Council whenever that member disagrees with a decision or action. If the member does not raise an issue with the Chairman, he is deemed to have agreed with the action or decision.

The Kolegium is strictly a peacetime organization. In the event of war, the Kolegium would no longer function and important issues would be handled directly by the Defense Council. During peacetime, the Kolegium, by operating as a "preliminary" Defense Council, takes part of the burden off the shoulders of the Defense Council and helps that organization run more smoothly. This helps explain why many people often mistakenly view the Kolegium as the Defense Council, rather than as the highest review and decision-rendering body in the Ministry of Defense.

Main Military Council. Another organization that would be dissolved when a war starts is the Main Military Council. This body is not a high-level decision-making organization, but rather an advisory body composed of a large group of military and Party, national and regional, officials, who have been appointed by the Minister of Defense and serve at his pleasure. Meeting three or four times a year, it is concerned mainly with questions of training, military uniforms, discipline, and so forth. Military councils exist in all commands down to Army level, and in each military council there is an official representative of some Party body.

General Staff. The General Staff is the "brain" of the armed forces. There is no counterpart in the United States. The Chairman of the General Staff presides over not only military decisions but civilian ones as well. For example, civilian capital and facility investments, such as hospitals and gas stations, require the approval of the Chief of the General Staff. He reviews all planned capital investments from the point of view of their possible contribution to Czechoslovak and Soviet defense plans to ensure that defense needs are adequately addressed in all such investments.

The General Staff is the main MOD organ bearing responsibility for the command and direction of military forces. The Chief of the General Staff is the First Deputy Minister of Defense. His responsibilities are:

- Long-term development of the Czechoslovak military forces.
- Development of socialist military science and doctrine.
- Preparation of military operations (Operation Plan) for defense of state territory.
- Organization of military forces and allocation of personnel and resources.
- Specification of the requirements for numbers and types of trained officers.
- Mobilization planning.
- Military readiness, which includes equipment, personnel, training, and so forth.
- Presentations to the Defense Council on the concept for the preparation of state territory for war.
- Preparation of the "special part of the state plan," which corresponds to the secret part of the budget, and of the development of the national economy for the needs of the military forces; thus, the Chief of the General Staff has to approve all "civilian" construction throughout the nation.
- Preparation of the mobilization plan for the supply of weapons, equipment, and materiel during wartime.
- Preparation of the request for the "untouchable" mobilization reserve, both civil and military (strategic reserve).
- Organization of the defense of the country against nuclear weapons.
- Identification and control of military and state secrets.
- Organization and control of military intelligence activity.
- Organization and provision of military technical assistance (terrorism and subversion) to other nations and subnational organizations, and of scientific and technological cooperation with allies.
- Participation in the preparation of the military budget, financial plan, and allocation among the military forces.

- Development of plans for cooperation with the Supreme High Command and all forces of the Warsaw Pact.
- Supervision over plans for civilian participation in the war.
- Representation of the Czechoslovak military forces in the Comecon.

Within the General Staff, the four most important administrations are Operations, Intelligence, Mobilization, and Material and Technical Supply. Plans for war are prepared within the Operations Administration of the Operations Department. Because of its duties, this body functions under very tight security: the only people with access to the whole Operation Plan are the head of the Operations Administration, members of the Operations Department, and the Defense Council. War plans are not allowed to leave this facility, and when the plans are reviewed by the Defense Council—a yearly process that takes place in the fall—it meets in the Operations Department's facility.

In the event of war, the Chief of the General Staff would describe the situation to the Defense Council and recommend what actions should be taken. Decisions of the Defense Council then would be translated into orders by its Secretary (that is, by the Chief of the General Staff) and transmitted directly to the forces and organizations.

5.
Communist Planning Process

AS INDICATED PREVIOUSLY, there are basically two types of decision-making in a communist system: decisions associated with short- and long-term plans, and emergency decisions. In the area of short- and long-term plans, three types are worthy of close examination: one-year plans that contain schedules and details; five-year plans that lay out an integrated political, economic, and military strategy and yearly goals; and long-term plans, those extending for more than five years—out to 15 years and beyond—that tend to deal more with global strategy.

In reviewing the planning process, it is important to recognize that all agencies, factories, ministries—organizations of all kinds—have plans, both one-year and five-year plans. All of the plans of similar nature run concurrently and are coordinated. The State Planning Commission is the key agency responsible for the organization of the planning process—except for the intelligence and the operation plans, to which the Commission does not have access. The Chief of the State Planning Commission is a member of the Defense Council and, in this capacity, does have access to the intelligence and operation plans. He is, therefore, the key individual in any conflicts or difficulties that might arise in the planning process. The main disputes that arise are generally between the Finance Minister and the Chief of the State Planning Commission, on one side, and the Minister of Defense, on the other.

One-Year Plans

The Czechoslovak and Soviet one-year plans run from January through December, and are prepared during the summer and fall for approval prior to the end of the year. The actual formal preparation of the schedule for Politburo, Defense Council, or Secretariat consideration and approval, as appropriate, is normally initiated in September. By then, specific goals have been set, inter-ministerial coordination and negotiation have been completed, and detailed schedules are being prepared. Each ministry prepares its own set of schedules. These are coordinated within the respective Central Committee departments and ultimately approved by department heads; they then submit these plans to the appropriate secretaries who, when satisfied, submit the plans to the Secretary General. In this process, it is important to note that the Administration and Organization departments report directly to the Secretary General and not through intermediate secretaries, as do the other departments.

When all schedules have been approved by the Secretary General, each department then provides its individual schedule to the Secretariat of the Secretary General, where all of them are merged together, coordinated, and, under the name of the Secretary General, presented to the Elected Secretariat and the Politburo for approval. Again, the Administration Department functions slightly differently in that its schedule is submitted to the Secretariat of the Chairman of the Defense Council, where it is summarized and submitted, under the name of the Secretary General, to the Defense Council for approval.

By this time, all inter-ministerial squabbles will have been resolved and final approval is usually a formality. The plans are approved and transmitted back to the appropriate ministers as orders based on decisions of the Secretariat, the Politburo, or the Defense Council, as appropriate, to carry out certain actions by specified dates. Also identified in the orders are the names of those specific individuals in other ministries and departments with whom each minister is to cooperate and the areas of cooperation.

In this manner, the one-year schedules are formally prepared, submitted, and reviewed. The same process is also followed during the summer, when the various goals for the departments are reviewed and approved and the schedules for accomplishment are confirmed or revised.

Five-Year Plans

The five-year plan utilizes quite a different approach, and it takes roughly two years to put it all together. This plan is probably best viewed as the integrated political, military, and economic strategy to be pursued over the next five years. The Politburo establishes a basic team comprised of 50 or so of the leading experts from all departments, ministries, and professional (especially scientific) organizations. The task of this team, which is normally headed by the Deputy Secretary General, is to work out the "guidelines" in all areas and disciplines. Set up within all of the departments are subteams, or task forces, which are led by members of the basic team. The members of these task forces are also appointed by the Politburo based upon department recommendations. In addition, representatives from appropriate related ministries and key individuals such as scientists serve on these task forces.

While the individual task forces normally operate within the various departments and hence within the organization shown in Figure 1, the overall team process takes place outside the organization. When its product is completed, it is submitted to the Politburo for approval. Since the mid-1950s, when the Party Congress was put on the same schedule as the five-year plan, one of its functions has been to give formal Party approval to the five-year plan. At the conclusion of the Party Congress, the individual ministers present to the Politburo, Elected Secretariat, or Defense Council, as appropriate, each minister's program for achieving the goals set forth in the five-year plan. This presentation usually takes the form of a 20-page document, which then becomes the basic guidance for the execution of the five-year plan.

State planners recognize that many events are unforeseen and can have a significant impact upon the five-year plan. When such changes or events take place, recommendations for changes to the five-year plan are made and submitted for approval to the body that originally approved the plan.

Long-Range Plans

Long-range planning extends well beyond five years and can be viewed, generally, as the development of global strategy. It is different from both of the preceding plans insofar as individual responsibilities are not spelled out. What is set forth, however, are the direction of the state and society and the goals to be achieved, often accompanied by specific dates, although the dates themselves are not that important.

Beginning in 1967, the East European countries were included in the Soviet long-range planning process—that is, in developing their own long-range plans to support the Soviet "Long-Range Strategic Plan for the Next 10-15 Years and the Years After." Top Party officials in each country received the basic Soviet analysis of the world situation together with those portions of the plan deemed important for each country to have in developing its own plan. Overall responsibility for Czechoslovak planning was assigned to the Deputy Secretary General, and the key organ in developing specialized plans was the Administration Department. Sejna, as First Secretary at the Ministry of Defense and a member of the Administration Department, had full access to the plan and was responsible for instructing the military in its preparations and for ensuring that the military portions properly reflected Party guidelines and goals.

The Soviet plan to which Sejna had access was composed of five main sections covering the basic assessment of the world situation, strategic goals, tactics, and responsibilities. The outline of the plan was as follows:

I. Analysis: An Overall Assessment of the World Situation
    Phases of Development
      1956-1959: Preparation for Peaceful Coexistence
      1960-1972: Peaceful Coexistence Struggle
      1973-1985: Period of Dynamic Social Change
      Thereafter: Global Democratic Peace

II. Strategic Goals: Global Focus
    Political Roles
        Communist Party
        Intelligence Services
        Diplomatic Services
        International Progressive Organizations
        Military Forces
        Anti-Socialist Forces
        Press/Media
        Political Relations with Third World Countries
        Religion
        Major Capitalist Alliances
        The Revolutionary Base
    Economy
        Energy
        Resources
        Agriculture
        War Industry
        Non-War Industry
        Finance System
        Welfare/Medical/Social Systems
        Third World Ties to Capitalist Countries
        Transportation and Communication
        National and International Corporations
        Research and Development
        Trade Between Socialist and Capitalist Countries
        Technical Information (Espionage)
    Military
        Correlation of Forces
        Peaceful Coexistence and its role in influencing or breaking down the military/industrial complex in capitalist countries.
        Exploitation of nationalist and anti-reactionary forces within various national military organizations (that is, how to exploit the military to strengthen pre-revolutionary or revolutionary movements in various countries around the world).
        Activities to be undertaken to discredit military defense forces in capitalist countries.

III. Tactics: How to Achieve the Goals

This section is first broken down by region, within regions by nations, and within nations by centers or bases from which the revolutionary forces can operate. Each element is examined in terms of its importance to Soviet political, economic, or military goals; the opportunity to bring about particular changes; and priorities. The regions addressed were:

  Western Europe
  United States/Canada
  Latin America
  Middle East
  Africa and Asia
IV. Individual Country Responsibilities
  Within this section various tasks are assigned to the individual socialist countries, and their activities are coordinated with those of the Soviet Union in pursuit of individual goals and tasks en route to strategic goals.
V. Socialist Country Development
  Within this section, again, political, military, and economic goals are identified and tactics are assigned for the achievement of these goals.

The Operation Plan

  The Operation Plan is the point of departure for understanding military planning as well as economic and social planning. Each section of the plan examines one variant of possible war. The types of variants that were considered in the mid- to late-1960s were:

- Global nuclear war: Soviet Union launches first.
- Global nuclear war: East and West launch simultaneously.
- Global nuclear war: the United States launches first.
- Local war with numerous countries participating: (1) in Scandinavia (assumes the United States is out of Europe); (2) in the Balkans (assumes the United States is out of Europe); (3) in Africa and the Middle East (arising from an oil supply crisis); and (4) a crisis over Berlin.
- Asia: the China problem.
- Conflicts triggered by counter-revolutionary movements, such as Czechoslovakia in 1968, requiring the assistance of other socialist states to restore order.

  The principal sections in the Czechoslovak Operation Plan, which is modeled after the Soviet plan, are as follows:

  1. Preamble. This sets forth the broad strategic view, which begins with a statement of the long-term, continuing goal of the coalition—i.e., the liquidation of capitalism—the coalition strategy to be pursued in achieving the overall objective, and the role of each satellite. Political and military goals are set forth, particularly the Czechoslovak operational contribution in support of these political and military goals.

2. The Main Tasks to Prepare the Country for War. This section contains the basic guidance on preparing various theaters for war. In this regard, it is assumed that Soviet and satellite forces are operating beyond their national borders. The section describes how the country must be prepared in all economic, political, and military aspects to go to war and specifies the time period within which the country, including the Party and the economy, must make the transition to a wartime operating posture. Guidelines are established for the number of men and women the country will call to arms, both in peace and war; the readiness of the forces; and the quantities of equipment, weapons, and supplies that will be required.

3. Force Posture and Major Missions. This section describes the capabilities of the armed forces needed to meet the requirements of the Operation Plan and wartime tasks. These forces consist of systems, such as infantry or tank divisions and air armies, and subsystems or undersystems, which in the West are called supporting elements, for example, engineer, communications, chemical, transportation, and artillery brigades.

In addition to setting forth the requirements for these units, this section establishes the manner in which each will participate in the Operation Plan. For example, it would specify the time at which the air army would bomb certain bases and intelligence operations would begin sabotage missions. The operational activity or tasks and general time schedule are set forth for each system and subsystem. In addition, the means for achieving coordination of all military operations, including those of other national forces, is prescribed.

4. System of Command. This section specifies the chain of command in a world war and the basic coordinating mechanisms, such as identification of attack axes, establishment of sector boundaries, and, in particular, specifications for targets and timing for employment of nuclear, chemical, and biological weapons, and sabotage. Identification of who has the authority to order use of different weapons is spelled out in this section.

5. Deployment and Dispersal Plan for Peace and War. Unit locations, both peacetime and secret wartime reserve locations, are identified. For the Second Strategic Echelon, collection points are also identified where various units would assemble and obtain their equipment prior to being transported to their reserve locations. Neighboring units and locations are also identified.

6. Organizational Plan for the Military Forces. This section provides a table of organization and equipment that spells out, down to battalion level, exactly how the Czechoslovak military organization is to be constituted in time of war, and also lists an inventory of available weapons and equipment. Coordination points both within Czechoslovak forces and between Czechoslovak forces and Soviet forces are set forth.

7. Preparation of the State Territory. The operational readiness of the national territory, including the support that is to be provided to other, non-Czechoslovak forces, is set forth. The types of preparations that are spelled out in this section include furbishing and stocking underground areas for occupation by troops under conditions of relocation and evacuation, and upgrading of various railroads, gas stations, airports, and other facilities, both for Czechoslovak and Soviet military forces.

8. Principles of Organization for Communications and Transportation. This part of the Operation Plan specifies principal and alternative transportation routes for Czechoslovak and Soviet troops in wartime. Communications between combat and territorial forces (mainly for supply), and between the Ministry of Defense and combat forces (especially for the supply of reserves) are set forth. Also included are plans for the restoration of destroyed communications.

9. Principles of Organization for Readiness and Mobilization. Within this section, the number of forces that are to be ready for combat and the schedules for their mobilization are spelled out. This includes the number of soldiers and officers, and related schedules and tables of equipment.

10. Information on the War Theater and Enemy Forces. This section provides maps which identify various facilities such as bridges and command posts. It also contains profiles of enemy forces—their training, firepower, morale, political preparation, and technical capability. Additionally, this section analyzes how NATO commanders are likely to react to various Pact initiatives, what their strategies are, and how NATO units have been trained to operate against Pact forces.

11. Civilian Evacuation Plan. Schedules, locations, and priorities are set forth for all civilians who are to be evacuated, and the factories, equipment, and other capital goods that can be moved. In this regard, preference is given to those people who can fight and work; the elderly and sick are generally ignored. Evacuation facilities include tunnels and mines and, in addition, areas where people and capital goods can be concealed, such as forests.

12. Principles of Political and Technical Preparation of the Occupied Territory. Instructions for governing territory seized from the enemy are spelled out from the occupying commander's point of view. They specify the form of government that is to be set up, and identify the individuals who are to be put into power, the local institutions that are to be used or eliminated, and the opposition leaders who are to be liquidated.

13. Activity of Military Counter-Intelligence Units. The types of actions which military counter-intelligence units and justice systems, from battalion level and up, can take are described in this section. These include political arrests, identification of people for deportation, and establishment of military justice and field courts that can render immediate decisions on persons in occupied territories.

14. Air Defense of the Territory. The national air defense system of the satellites is completely integrated with the Soviet national air defense (PVO Strany), with Czechoslovak air defenses covering not only the homeland but portions of Poland as well. Czechoslovak units report directly to and receive orders from the Soviet air defense commander. The integrated system coverage and command organization is set forth in this section.

15. Operation of Strategic Intelligence and Sabotage (Diversion) Units. This plan details how strategic intelligence operations in the civilian and military services are to be combined in war, provides directives for the timing and targets of sabotage in enemy territory, and identifies the units and equipment to be allocated for each sabotage mission.

16. Civil Defense. All aspects of civil defense are addressed in this section, including defense against paratroops, counter-revolutionaries, and sabotage, as well as plans for evacuation, reconstruction, and the provision of medical aid.

17. Research and Development. This section contains instructions for determining research and development priorities during wartime, especially with regard to weapons, and plans for dealing with critical production problems.

18. Money/Finances During the War. Instructions on the payment of soldiers in wartime are set forth here.

19. Directions for Preparation of Czechoslovak Military Forces. This section deals with the readiness of Czechoslovak military forces and the emphasis that should be placed on training in, for example, night operations, bad weather conditions, offense as opposed to defense, nuclear as opposed to conventional warfare.

20. Political Plans. This is normally the last section in the Operation Plan, and is prepared by the Main Political Administration and Military Intelligence Administration (GRU). It describes how wartime operations are to be presented to the soldiers on the battlefield, to the people in occupied territories, and to the rest of the world. Cover, deception, and disinformation activities are set forth; the Party organs involved in the operation are identified; and the missions of radio, television, and press are described. Such items as ration cards and new money for use in occupied territories are addressed.

Preparing the Operation Plan

The development of the Operation Plan is clearly a very sensitive and tightly controlled process. Only the highest military and Party leaders are cleared for access to the whole plan, together with the very few officials—14 in Czechoslovakia—who work on the plan on a day-to-day basis. These include the chiefs of the Operations Administration and the Operations Department, and 12 officers who are carefully selected for the Operations Department. These individuals are clearly destined for high military position. The Chief of the Operations Administration is Deputy to the Chief of Staff; in Czechoslovakia he has three deputies, while in the Soviet Union he has at least five. His first deputy is also chief of the Operations Department, which prepares the whole plan and organizes the work of other people in agencies whose contributions must be coordinated with the plan—for example, the Mobilization Administration. The heads and chiefs of staff of these other agencies are the only persons in these agencies who are allowed to go to the Operations Department and work on their part of the plan—and only their part.

It is important not to confuse this Operations Administration with the Department of Operations Preparation, which is the organization responsible for such matters as war games, troop maneuvers, and training exercises at the operational level (army) and higher.

Numerous charts, maps, and tables are used in the operations room for assessing the preparation for war of the military and the country and reporting to the Defense Council. The types of maps and charts that are used include:

- Maps that show the locations of units during peacetime and wartime.
- Mobilization charts for troops and equipment.

- Mobilization charts of the national economy identifying all factories and units that would switch to a wartime mobilization basis, and the timing of this action.
- Charts of military organization in wartime and how the transition from a peacetime footing is accomplished (an area where there may be significant problems).
- Targets that are covered by intelligence agents when the war starts.
- Charts describing the troop material supply system (everything from weapons to food, footwear, and uniforms).
- Political organization charts, identifying persons and, of particular importance, communications such as television, radio, and mobile units that would be instrumental in governing various countries in time of war.
- Charts assessing enemy firepower.
- Tables of nuclear weapons effects: the damage which Soviet nuclear strikes could do to enemy forces, and the damage which enemy nuclear strikes could do to Soviet forces.
- Evacuation plans and time-tables.
- Organizational charts for transportation, particularly with regard to the supply of important materials and forces.
- Charts detailing sabotage operations.

The Operation Plan is revised annually: Each March the plan for the coming year is approved and preparation of a new one for the subsequent year is begun. In February or March, the Defense Council in the Soviet Union approves the guidelines for the next Operation Plan. These contain the basic requirements around which the plan is to be designed: for example, the speed of the attack, the use of parachute units, the type of tanks that would be used, and so forth. The Chief of the Soviet General Staff calls his Czechoslovak counterpart and gives him the requirements to be met in the new plan. For example, in the next Operation Plan, Czechoslovak military forces might be required to mobilize 35 rather than 30 divisions, the speed of the attack might be increased, and they might be given instructions to use parachute units in support of division-level operations.

The key people involved in putting together the Operation Plan are the Chief of the General Staff and the Operations Department, which in Czechoslovakia in 1968 consisted of 12 people in addition to the Chief and was organizationally attached to the Operations Administration. This group is responsible for preparing the guidelines that will be presented to the Czechoslovak Defense Council for planning approval.

Documents prepared in this process—guidelines, schedules, and plans—never leave the General Staff area and, in particular, the operations room, or, as it is referred to, the SAL. In developing the guidelines, all commanders of forces and special forces—i.e., army, air force, chemical troops, engineer troops, and so forth—participate, but each has access only to his part of the plan, and each must do his work at General Staff Headquarters, that is, it cannot be done in his own office. The only people with full access to this process are members of the Operations Department. Even military counter-intelligence officers who are in charge of security cannot go into the SAL. In addition to the Operations Department personnel, only the members of the Defense Council itself, which is the STAVKA in wartime, can go into the SAL.

The Minister of Defense personally participates in drawing up the plan, focusing his attention primarily on aspects of troop control—in particular, how to accomplish the element of surprise and how to control front operations. Toward the end of the planning year, the Minister of Defense usually spends a half day a week in the SAL.

The Operation Plan has a major impact on the economy and society, because the planning process frequently shows the need for such items as new or improved roads and bridges and such weapons as new missiles and tanks. This interaction between military needs and the economy emerges as a major confrontation (usually from late December to February) between the Minister of Defense and the Chief of the State Planning Commission—a contest between orders contained in the guidelines received from the Soviet Defense Council and realistic possibilities as analyzed by the State Planning Commission. The Secretary General himself is often called upon to resolve these disagreements, and this intervention may occur several times in this two-month period. When the differences have been settled, the Defense Council meets in the Operations Department of the General Staff Headquarters where it discusses and approves the plan.

The Operation Plan is approved and signed by the Secretary General, as Chairman of the Defense Council. Pertinent sections of it then percolate—usually in April—down through the military chain of command to the lower levels. The Chief of the General Staff approves the plans that go to each military district, and the chief of staff of each military district then approves the various sections that go to the armies, and so forth. At the State Planning Commission, the Operation Plan is put into the economic planning process, which begins in the summer. As various plans are developed throughout the year, those that have been fitted into the Operation Plan are so indicated by a statement on the front cover.

Military counter-intelligence and civilian secret police are involved to a certain extent in the planning process and may make recommendations on the plan to the Secretary General as it is being formulated. They become more actively involved when the plan is approved and transmitted for implementation. Military counter-intelligence officers are concerned from the point of view of secrecy, information security, and internal sabotage. The civilian secret police from the economic section of the Ministry of Interior—they are essentially economic or technical experts, not security experts—have the task of control against sabotage. Their anti-sabotage function is to conduct constant reviews of the projects and identify any assignments that are not being implemented properly.

Once the Operation Plan is approved, the Chief of the General Staff, not the Minister of Defense, has control over the plan. He decides what weapons and equipment are to be purchased, which roads get repaired, and so forth. All civil improvement programs, such as road, gas station, hospital, and school construction, are sent to the Chief of the General Staff for his review and approval, veto, or modification. Also participating in this process is the military section of the Committee of State Control.

The Inspector General within the Ministry of Defense also has a major role. With the exception of the Operations Department and its SAL, the Inspector General can go anywhere in the conduct of his duties. His responsibility is to review the delivery of such military items as guns, tanks, and missiles, the readiness of units to receive these materials, and their production at factories. He wields considerable power over both military and civilian agencies and reports directly to the Minister of Defense and through the Administration Department to the Defense Council on problems that he identifies. Within the Committee of State Control there is also a military section that is responsible for reviewing the implementation of Defense Council decisions within the civilian sector.

Party organizations also participate in special areas. For example, they may investigate to determine whether directives issued to, say, the Chemical Troops are carried out. Any discrepancies or problems would be reported to the First Secretary of the Party at the Ministry of Defense, a position Sejna held from 1964 on. The First Secretary then could take his recommendation for appropriate action to the Minister of Defense, or to the Secretary General, although in the latter case he would most likely go through the Administration Department of the Central Committee. Additionally, the Disciplinary Committee could be used to discipline or punish any military officer or civilian employee of the Ministry of Defense who was found to be responsible for the problem.

Material Technical Supply Plan

After the Operation Plan is approved, which normally occurs in the early part of the year, the Material and Technical Supply Administration of the General Staff identifies the capabilities—troops, reserves, other personnel, equipment, weapons, transportation, and communications, and their state of readiness—required to accomplish the specified missions. This Administration coordinates its efforts with the Military Administration of the State Planning Commission to determine what can or cannot be provided; the head of the latter body establishes priorities and resolves the problems, and then sends a report on the completed requirements to the Defense Council. The strategy for technology research and development and production is developed by the General Staff to meet the requirements of the Operations Department. The General Staff also retains the lead role in the development of long-range technical plans.

Based on these requirements, the secret portion of the plan and budget is formulated by the Military Administration of the State Planning Commission, the Military Department of the Treasury, the Finance Administration of the Ministry of Defense where a special department prepares the secret portion of the military budget, and the General Staff.

Mobilization Plan

There are three levels of mobilization: (1) total mobilization; (2) limited mobilization, involving portions of the reserves whose mission is of more immediate importance; and (3) selective mobilization, under which only specialists such as intelligence and parachute units and some officers would be called up. In the case of mobilization of both the economy and the armed forces, the Mobilization Plan specifies the times, places, and mechanisms (e.g., alerting, call up, transport) whereby the forces are marshaled for an all-out war effort.

The Mobilization Plan sets forth the detailed organization of the military forces in peace and war, the allocation of weapons and equipment, materials to be supplied by the civilian sector, the peacetime and wartime location of military units, the system for calling reserves into service, the plan for the supply of troops in war, and so forth. Relocation, camouflage of units, diplomatic missions to cover mobilization activity, and plans for transferring units from collection points to reserve positions are all specified. Of particular importance is the planning for the strategic and state reserves.[3]

Mobilization in the Soviet Union and Warsaw Pact countries has both military and civilian aspects. They are equally important and closely coordinated. Within the civilian side of the plan, mobilization reserves (those immediately required for war) are identified and the schedules for the transition of both individuals and industries to military tasks are specified. An especially important part of the mobilization plan prescribes the reorganization of the Party and government offices and the focus of wartime authority. Certain organs (e.g., elected ones) cease to exist, new laws come into effect, and new authorities (e.g., political commissars) are specified. These

---

[3] Strategic reserves are those reserves essential for the continuing conduct of war. State reserves are less important, oriented toward the needs of the population. Strategic reserves are also state reserves.

processes all take time and introduce certain problems or vulnerabilities. Consequently, an analysis of this activity is important to an understanding of how the Soviets go to war, the speed with which they can make the transition to a wartime basis, and the vulnerabilities that arise in the process, both in the Soviet Union and in the East European nations.

Mobilization administrations or departments exist in all organizations, both military and civilian, down to the regional level. Each factory, farm, television station, transportation unit, and so forth has a "special" department called ZO (Zvlástni Oddéleni) which is composed mainly of reserve or retired military officers who prepare the mobilization plan for each factory, farm, and so forth. Industrial and mobilization plans detail the new military items that specific plants will produce, the rate of production that is demanded, the people who will staff the plants and thus are exempt from the draft, the wartime locations of plants (they are relocated on the eve of war), and the equipment and raw materials that are prepositioned as part of the strategic reserve. The line of authority for mobilization matters extends up through the military chain of command to the Mobilization Administration in the General Staff, which directs the overall effort. These special departments (ZOs) are also in charge of secrecy in their own organizations and in this function are controlled by the secret police.

6.
Control and Oversight

Personnel and Career Progression

PERSONNEL ADVANCEMENT, like other aspects of the communist system, stresses organization, planning, and oversight. Career progression is carefully orchestrated. Over the years, there have been numerous reports in the West of favoritism and nepotism within the Soviet hierarchy, and undoubtedly this is true, as it is in any system. But this should not be confused with incompetence or unpreparedness. The communist system is designed to develop cadres of trained people for all positions. As the political system matures and stabilizes, it becomes unusual to find people in responsible jobs who do not possess adequate experience or knowledge for those jobs. Moreover, if a person does not perform satisfactorily, further advancement is unlikely.

The organizational concept responsible for ensuring an adequate supply of reliable individuals to fill positions is the Cadres Reserve. In the military, the top organization is the Main Cadres Administration. This administration deals with division and higher level appointments. For each organization, such as Tank Troops, Engineers, and so forth, a Plan of Cadres Reserves is prepared. The purpose of this plan is to ensure the constant availability of three candidates ready and qualified to step in and take over each position should something happen to the incumbent—transfer, death, arrest, illness. The plans identify by name the individuals, their backgrounds and qualifications; if additional preparation such as schooling is deemed important, the appropriate activity is scheduled. As a consequence of this process, positions rarely go unfilled for lack of a qualified, available person. The process also produces a natural competition for each position. And each person has a reasonably definite, and known, career progression established.

In any position, an individual's performance is carefully observed by a number of persons with oversight responsibility—and, in addition, by often jealous co-workers. The most important oversight is provided by the command chain, that is, by superiors. Second, the Party group or political commissar evaluates the individual's ideology and Party loyalty. Third, military or civilian counter-intelligence keeps watch for possible sabotage or treason. Fourth, the Main Cadres Administration, or the union in the case of a civilian, examines job performance. And fifth, an official in the appropriate Party department that has nomenklatura over the individual is in constant touch with the individual and plans his or her career.

Several times each year, each individual meets with some Party official, depending on who holds his nomenklatura, to review his progress and performance and examine career opportunities. This adviser/Party-evaluator discusses with the individual such topics as advanced schooling, promotions, subsequent assignment, and the Cadres Reserve list that the individual is on. In the case of senior military officers or intelligence officers, the key Party department is the Administration Department.

Every two years and prior to every change in position, promotion, or assignment to an educational institution, an appraisal committee is formed to review an individual's accomplishments, performance, and future prospects. The appraisal committee is chaired by a Party department official and includes the individual's superior commander or supervisor, the political commissar, and a Party official. Each time this appraisal is performed, a different official conducts the interview. During the interview, past performance is reviewed, the individual's strengths and weaknesses are discussed, and agreement is reached on future directions. The basic conclusion reached might be, for example: "The candidate has been successful and we recommend he continue as previously planned—and for his next assignment . . . ." These plans often look twenty years into the future. And from the other direction, when someone is selected for a position, it is most unusual for that person not to have had a long progression of work and educational experiences that have directly prepared the person for the job. If the individual is displeased with the results of the appraisal, he or she may appeal to higher authority.

Throughout this process, the most important oversight is performed by the official from the particular Party department. In the case of an employee in the military, secret police, and justice, the Administration Department, as previously mentioned, has nomenklatura for the position, and individual, at issue.

This process is not unique to the military; it applies to the entire state structure—government, Party, engineers, technicians, scientists, teachers, physicians, lawyers, and so forth. This is another reason why the communist system needs to be considered in its entirety as a militant system.

Nomenklatura

Nomenklatura is the name for the system which gives the Party control over individuals in specific positions. Every job in the communist empire comes under the control of some Party body. That Party body has the power to appoint individuals to, and to dismiss them from, specific positions, and it has authority over individuals in those positions, including, for example, their training, education, travel, and promotions. This power is nomenklatura.

Nomenklatura recently has been associated in many Western studies with a list of top positions or with the Party elite in the communist system. This characterization is misleading, because *everyone* in the communist system, from city to regional, state and federal levels, belongs to some Party official's nomenklatura. In the Ministry of Defense, for example, the generals (and marshals in the Soviet Union) come under the nomenklatura of the Politburo; the Minister himself belongs to the Central Committee; officers at the level of colonel belong to the military section of the Administration Department; and officers below the rank of colonel belong to the nomenklatura of the First Secretary of the Main Party Committee at the Ministry of Defense—who was Sejna from 1964 to 1968.

While this oversight and control exist at all levels, there are two distinct breaks or hierarchies in the system. The first is encountered when one's nomenklatura is held by one of the departments of the Central Committee; at this level, the individual is said to have broken into the inner circle. The second, when it is held by the Politburo or Central Committee itself; in this case, the individual is within the innermost circle, where Party politics and loyalties play the determining roles. At the same time, when the Central Committee or Politburo holds nomenklatura, it is still the departments and secretaries who wield the main influence. The departments, in particular, keep watch over the positions and incumbents on a daily basis for the Politburo and Central Committee. Moreover, it is the departments or secretaries, especially the Elected Secretariat, that recommend promotions to the Politburo, or through the Politburo to the Central Committee. Central Committee and Politburo action on positions is, as indicated earlier, mainly a rubber-stamp, pro forma action. Selected examples of upper echelon positions, the base of their nomenklatura, and the location of the actual power of selection are presented in Figure 5.

This diagram demonstrates why the power of the Party is said to be concentrated in the Party apparatus, especially in the Secretariat and the departments. People often say that in the communist system power is divided among the Party, the military, and the secret police (i.e., StB in Czechoslovakia, KGB in the Soviet Union). As a first order approximation, this is correct, but it is not entirely accurate. First, it is the Party apparatus, not the whole Party, that wields the power, and, within this apparatus, the Secretariat has the real power. And second, it is important to understand that the Party is the most important of the three "equals" because the Party is able to manipulate the military and the secret police.

FIGURE 5
Organizational Nomenklatura for Selected High Level Positions

POSITIONS	NOMENKLATURA
Secretary General	Central Committee
Deputy Secretary General	Central Committee
Central Committee Secretaries	Central Committee
Politburo	Central Committee
Elected Secretariat	Central Committee
Chairman, State Planning Commission	Central Committee
Ministers	Central Committee
Central Committee Control and Revision Commissions	Central Committee
Chairman, Main Political Administration	Politburo
Deputy Chairman, Main Political Administration	Politburo
Generals and Marshals	Politburo
Chief of General Staff	Politburo
Commanders of Military Districts	Politburo
Deputy Minister of Defense and Service Chiefs	Politburo
Parliament	Politburo
General Staff Administration Heads	Politburo
Government Head of Administration	Politburo
First Secretaries at Ministries	Politburo
Kolegium	Politburo
Head Military Administration at	Politburo
State Planning Commission	
Finance	
Party Control	
Presidium of Parliament	Politburo
Deputy Ministers	Politburo
Ambassadors	Politburo
Central Committee Department Heads	Elected Secretariat
Party Group Leaders	Elected Secretariat
First Secretaries at Ministries	Elected Secretariat
Central Committee Department/Section Chiefs	Elected Secretariat
State and Regional First Secretaries	Elected Secretariat
Administration Department	Defense Council
Administration Department Section	Defense Council
Kolegium at Ministry of Defense	Defense Council
Kolegium at STB	Defense Council
Central Committee Department Staffs	Party Committee at Central Committee

Decision Implementation Oversight

An important dimension of the decision process is control over implementation. Provision for control is incorporated into every decision that anyone makes in the Soviet Union.

The key organizations in implementing decisions are the departments. When the Central Committee, Politburo, Secretariat, or Defense Council makes a decision, each department involved or affected by that decision makes what is called a work organization, which is a plan for implementing the decision. After the political directives are approved and handed down, they are to be implemented within the various ministries. Any changes to these plans have to be approved by the Party bodies that were involved in making the original decision. In matters dealing with national security, changes would have to be approved by the Administration Department and by the Defense Council. In matters handled by the International Department, changes would have to be approved by the Secretariat and the Defense Council or the Politburo, depending upon the nature of the change.

The key role of the departments in implementing decisions is in providing guidance on the precise meaning of the decisions to those officials (e.g., ministers) who have the task of preparing the implementation plans. These plans consist principally of time schedules and specification of interministerial coordination that are presented to and approved by the department at the appropriate time—for example, one to three months following the rendering of the decision by the Politburo, Secretariat, or Defense Council.

When a decision, for instance, emanates from the Defense Council, the head of the Administration Department would call on the Minister of Defense, the Chief of the General Staff, the Chief of the Main Political Administration, the First Secretary of the Party within the Ministry of Defense, and other ministers and officers as appropriate, for example, the Foreign or Interior Minister. The head of the Administration Department reviews the Defense Council decision with these individuals, elaborating and clarifying the various paragraphs. He then orders the various ministers, chiefs, and so forth, to carry out whatever tasks are necessary under the decision of the Defense Council. The principal control mechanisms of the Administration Department over the MOD are shown in Figure 4.

The variety of controls that are established from the beginning depend heavily on the type of decisions and agencies involved. In general, decisions by the Politburo, Secretariat, or Defense Council have three main controls that are exercised through the Ministry of Interior, the Party, and the government. In addition, the departments themselves establish their own mechanisms for following the progress of implementation.

In the case of important decisions, Party control, oversight, and discipline are exercised through the Control and Revision Commission of the Central Committee. In the military forces, this is done through the Control and Revision Commission of the Main Political Administration. Similar commissions exist as part of the Central Committee apparatus down to the regional level. The Commission in Czechoslovakia has two sections, one that controls the use of Party money, and one that oversees the implementation of decisions of the highest Party bodies. (In the Soviet Union, there are two separate commissions.) Commission officials have the authority to go to any ministry or any factory and inspect the manner in which decisions of the Politburo, Central Committee, parliament, government, and so forth are being carried out. Where they are displeased with the process of implementation, they are responsible for recommending disciplinary measures to the appropriate body that holds nomenklatura. This control and discipline is normally exercised by the Commission at levels below that of secretaries and department heads.

The Administration Department also directs the Ministry of Interior to follow various aspects of the implementation process. The civilian secret police monitor those aspects outside the Ministry of Defense: military counter-intelligence, which is an arm of the Ministry of Interior, not the GRU, monitors the appropriate aspects within the Ministry of Defense and defense industry.

Progress is monitored on behalf of the government by the Ministry of State Control, which reports directly to the Prime Minister. This monitoring function is coordinated with the Control and Revision Commission by having the Minister of State Control sit on this body. This process is followed for all Politburo and Secretariat decisions.

In the case of Defense Council decisions, progress is monitored in a slightly different manner because of the classified nature of the work involved: The Ministry of Defense has an Inspector General (IG) who works jointly for the Central Committee and the Minister of Defense. This IG also has authority to inspect civilian organs concerned with the implementation of Defense Council decisions. Within each ministry, there is a Party Committee or political department, which has a bureau that operates as a lower-level counterpart of the Politburo. The First Secretary of the Party Committee is chairman of this bureau, which, in addition to monitoring progress, has a direct review and approval responsibility. The Defense Ministry in Czechoslovakia has two bureaus, one specifically dealing with intelligence, the other, with all other appropriate issues. In the Soviet Ministry of Defense there are six bureaus, with one attached to each of the major sections; namely, Air Force, Navy, Ground Forces, Strategic Rocket Forces, General Staff, and Intelligence. The most important communist officials in each section are members of these individual bureaus. Plans for implementation of decisions are drawn up and presented to these bureaus, which review the decisions and make recommendations or changes, as appropriate, and monitor progress within the Ministry.

The Main Political Administration (MPA) of the military forces is an especially important control organ. This Administration is *not* subordinate to the Minister of Defense. Rather, it should be viewed as an arm of the Administration Department that operates as a department of the Central Committee. The MPA has a bureau—as the Central Committee has a Politburo—which functions as a collective political organ that meets every week to examine and discuss the major political tasks in the military forces and, if appropriate, report back to the Secretariat or Defense Council. In his capacity as First Secretary at the MOD, Sejna was also a member of the MPA bureau. The MPA Chief also can report directly to the Secretary General.

The Main Political Administration is organized almost like a miniature Central Committee, but without the economic departments. The First Administration in the MPA is almost like the Party Organization Department and directs all Party activity inside the military forces. The Second Administration is responsible for ideology. There is a Third Administration of propaganda, agitation, press, and culture. The Fourth is the Cadres or Personnel Administration. Of special importance is the Fifth Administration which handles special propaganda, a cover name for disinformation and deception. There is also, as noted above, a Control and Revision Commission that handles money and discipline in a manner similar to its counterpart in the Central Committee.

7.
Case Studies of Decision-Making

Deployment of Anti-Aircraft Missiles into Czechoslovakia in the Early 1960s

BY LETTER, Soviet leader Khrushchev informed the First Secretary of Czechoslovakia that the Soviet Union would provide anti-aircraft missiles to bolster Czechoslovak defenses. These were to be paid for by Czechoslovakia. The Minister of Defense and the Chief of the General Staff were summoned to Moscow for a secret meeting to receive instructions regarding this deployment. In Moscow, the Soviet Minister of Defense, Malinovskiy, ordered them to prepare bases within three months and to send the Czechoslovak missile specialists, who had received training the previous year in the Soviet Union, back for further instructions.

Upon their return to Prague, the Minister of Defense and Chief of the General Staff, together with the Minister of Interior, prepared a short (about a six-page) proposal which was submitted to the Defense Council describing how that body should proceed. This proposal contained recommendations for the issuance of Defense Council orders to the most important officials: the Minister of Defense, Finance Minister, Chief of the State Planning Commission, Foreign Trade Minister, Minister of Interior (StB), and chief of the Administration Department. These orders called for the preparation of a joint decision document for the Defense Council. The Administration Department was charged with coordinating the preparation of this planning document. Also spelled out in the orders were the principles of security governing the preparation of the Joint Planning Document. Finally, by decision of the Defense Council, the orders took the form of an emergency decision outside the normal economic plan. As a consequence of this decision, officials were given the power in developing the joint plan to identify reserves of monies and other resources that could be used to underwrite project costs and to estimate the size of loans from the Soviet Union that might be needed.

Fourteen days were allocated to the preparation of the planning document for presentation to the Defense Council. The document was written under the leadership of the Chief of the General Staff, with the participation of only the Technical Administration (Military Department) at the Foreign Trade Ministry, the State Planning Commission, and the Ministry of Finance. The Technical Administration is the group that negotiates weapons sales with foreign nations. All participants in the planning exercise were specifically approved, by name, by the Defense Council.

As written, the Joint Planning Document identified schedules and decisions for Defense Council action. The locations of the bases were selected, and appropriate orders were drawn up for the Minister of Agriculture to set aside the necessary land areas. Guidelines for providing special security were contained in orders to the Minister of Interior (military counter-intelligence). Also specified were the criteria to be applied in the selection of officers, soldiers, and civilians—and their families—who would be constructing the bases. The document also contained orders for the Minister of Foreign Trade regarding the method of paying for the missiles. In this case, the Minister of Foreign Trade was directed to seek a loan from the Soviet Union to finance the entire operation because at that time Czechoslovakia had no reserve funds.

Directives for transporting the missiles to their Czech bases and for camouflaging the entire operation were set forth. From start to finish, all operations, sites, and activities were to be kept secret. Security was extremely tight. For example, when construction of the first base was completed and ready for inspection, members of the Politburo and the Kolegium of the Ministry of Defense were taken to the site in a bus whose windows were covered to ensure that none of them would know where the site was located.

Construction of the bases was accomplished in roughly three months and the missiles arrived about one month later. Each base accommodated one missile battalion, with conventional warheads.

The project was controlled by both the Czechoslovaks and the Soviets. Soviet control was exercised by seven construction engineers who supervised the building of the bases and by twelve military counter-intelligence (KGB) officers. They were provided three offices at the Czechoslovak military counter-intelligence headquarters; in addition to reporting to their appropriate control in the Soviet Union, they had direct access to the Chief of the Czechoslovak General Staff. As indicated, all Czechoslovak construction workers, officers, and Party members alike who were to work on the project were individually approved by the Defense Council, and this was true also of the Czechoslovak military counter-intelligence officers who provided part of the oversight control function.

Knowledge of the operation was on a strict need-to-know basis. While the Administration Department was responsible for this operation, only the head of this department and his deputy knew what was happening. Within the Ministry of Interior, the head of military counter-intelligence was involved in the operation; and a special group was created that reported both to the head of military counter-intelligence and directly to the Chief of the General Staff. The latter was the individual responsible for security. Within the Ministry of Defense, knowledge was restricted to the military construction organization and to the chief of anti-aircraft artillery. Within the Finance Ministry, only the Military Administration was informed; within the State Planning Commission, only the Military Administration; and within the Foreign Trade Ministry, only the Military Department (which was referred to by its cover name, the Technical Administration). The Ministry of Agriculture knew nothing about the operation—only what lands it was to set aside.

The Shift From Defense to Offense in 1963

The Soviet decision on this major strategic shift was communicated "unofficially" by Marshal Malinovskiy in May 1963 when he met in Prague with the twelve members of the Kolegium of the Ministry of Defense. Malinovskiy informed the Kolegium that the Soviet Union was ready to make this transition and that Czechoslovakia, which provided important first strategic echelon forces, would also make the transition and would have to adhere to the Soviet schedule. At this meeting he identified the three ways in which the next war might be initiated: (1) missiles are launched first by the West, (2) missiles pass each other overhead, and (3) missiles are launched first by the East. He asserted that the first two cases were unacceptable to the Kremlin, and that, henceforth, a major effort would be directed toward preparations for launching a surprise attack against the enemy. In this regard, he pointed out, military readiness and deception would play the most important roles.

The following month, in June, the First Secretary and Minister of Defense of Czechoslovakia were called to a meeting of the Political Consultative Committee (the highest-ranking Warsaw Pact political and military decision-making organization) in Moscow where Khrushchev explained the new policy and Marshal Grechko laid out the details.

Following this meeting, the Czechoslovak First Secretary submitted to the Defense Council under his signature a report that had been prepared by Sejna and the Administration Department. In addition to recommending orders which the Defense Council could use to set in motion the necessary military reforms, this report specified the information that could be made available to the whole Politburo—an important matter in this case, since a major decision such as this one could not be kept completely secret, and thus guidelines were required regarding what the Politburo was permitted or needed to know. The Defense Council orders were transmitted to the Minister of Defense and the chief of the Administration Department, instructing them to prepare documents for Defense Council approval that would cover all changes in the Czechoslovak military necessitated by the Soviet decision, e.g., the operation and mobilization plans, training, finance, and so forth.

In preparation for this activity, the Minister of Defense sent a military delegation, headed by the Chief of the Czechoslovak General Staff, to Moscow where its members spent more than a week receiving instructions and information from their counterparts in the Soviet military. Upon their return, a new document was prepared for the Defense Council by the Minister of Defense under the leadership of the Chief of the General Staff. The document opened with a justification of the project: In summary, because of new developments in technology, increases in force strength, and especially the importance of strategic goals, Czechoslovak leaders considered it absolutely essential to take a number of measures to strengthen the country's military posture.

For Czechoslovakia, the most important part of the document was the question of money. It was clear that the current Czechoslovak defense budget could not support these new requirements and that the military buildup would have to be underwritten by increased revenues. These increases would be substantial, for the new tasks encompassed the development of a civil defense system as well as preparations for offensive operations with the latter including requirements for many new roads, other transportation lines, underground command/control facilities, and supply depots. The estimated cost to Czechoslovakia for these improvements was one billion krona every year, which would make the per capita costs for defense in Czechoslovakia higher than it was at the time in the United States.

The Defense Council directed all involved agencies and parties to prepare new plans for its approval in accordance with a strict schedule. Some of the more important plans and budgets that were to be developed concerned the items mentioned above, such as civil defense and improvements to transportation and communication systems, a new Operation Plan, the design of deceptive propaganda to cover the changes, and education and training of the military, including the improvement of morale. The Administration Department was assigned the responsibility of controlling the entire process, which began in the fall of 1963 in the Ministry of Defense when all officers returned to Prague to learn about the plan for the coming year. At this meeting, not only the Minister of Defense but also the First Secretary of the Communist Party emphasized the significance of the undertaking.

In contrast to the anti-aircraft missile deployment example, this was a fundamental, long-term change; hence, controls and review processes were set up not in an ad hoc manner, but as part of the normal control regime. The overall review process was assigned by the Defense Council to the Minister of Defense, the Chief of the Main Political Administration, and the Minister of Interior (military counter-intelligence), who were directed to present reports on the readiness of the new military plan to the Defense Council twice each year. In this review, they were to report on the progress achieved in introducing changes, of which one of the most important was progress in the education of officers.

The Militarization of Society in the mid-1960s

While it is often advertised that the Party Congress is the top decision-making body, this is not accurate because it fails to take into account the interaction of the Soviet planning process with that of Czechoslovakia. This was nowhere made more clearly apparent than in a simple sentence in the Czechoslovak Party report of the 13th Party Congress in June 1966 concerning "the need to build a united defense system." This passage had major implications, for it reflected Soviet instructions to Czechoslovakia to introduce major changes in conformance with the new Soviet offensive strategy.

After the Congress adjourned, all ministries and central offices established high-level committees to meet and come to an understanding of what "building a united defense system" meant and what their contributions would be. In the Ministry of Defense, the committee was headed by the deputy of the Chief of the General Staff. In all committees the respective department heads, or their deputies, participated. Each committee was to prepare a document for the Politburo, Secretariat, or Defense Council, as appropriate, on the role of their ministry. Many of these committees established subcommittees to address special topics (e.g., in the Ministry of Defense, there were subcommittees on rear services, radiotechnology, chemical warfare, transportation, etc.). Participation on these committees and subcommittees was not delegated; on the contrary, the review process involved the highest ranking officials for 12 to 16 hours a day over a two-month period.

At the beginning, the Administration Department, which already knew what the Party meant by "building a united defense system," met with all participants to explain the meaning of the phrase and to be sure that the committees understood their tasks. The undertaking, as laid out at this meeting, encompassed a broad range of subjects, including the training and education of children from six years on; production and manning schedules for everything from collective farms and light industry up to heavy industry; the building and repairing of highways, railroads, and airports; and improvements to command and organizational structures, and the system of control in the military forces.

When the reports received from each of the ministries and central offices were assembled, the resulting document was presented to the Kolegium of the Ministry of Defense—consisting of, as Chairman, the Minister of Defense, and, as members, the Chief of the General Staff, all MOD deputy ministers, the chief of the Main Political Administration, the chief of the Personnel Administration, and the First Secretary of the Party at the

Ministry of Defense. The appropriate bureaucrats from the military section of the Administration Department were included as observers. This organization does not exist in wartime; it is basically a peacetime coordination group. The final review of the document was a two-day, 24-hour meeting in which all sections were carefully reviewed by this group. Subsequently, it went to the Defense Council where all the guidelines were approved and directions were handed down to all ministries and central offices to prepare detailed plans for the Defense Council.

The Process of Converting Castro's Cuba into a Marxist-Leninist State

The Cuban Revolution that brought Fidel Castro to power on January 1, 1959, is a good example of Soviet tactics in operation. The essence of these tactics is to support nationalist revolutionary movements, infiltrate them but maintain a covert presence, and then, as soon as possible after the revolution has succeeded, to take control and turn it to "socialism."

Prior to the consummation of the revolution, Fidel Castro was not a member of the Cuban Communist Party. There was considerable distrust between him and the Soviets, who regarded Fidel as being too far to the left and referred to him as an anarchist. The Soviets also did not trust Fidel because he was the son of a capitalist; as such, according to Moscow, he could never really accept communism. This is why he was not "elected" to the Politburo of the Cuban Communist Party, even after he took power, and why he was referred to as the Prime Minister, not the First Secretary, for many years. In return, Castro did not trust the Soviets, and upon occasion, even had top Party officials arrested for passing confidential information to their East European comrades (i.e., for spying).

In early 1959, after Castro was in command, he approached Czechoslovakia for military aid and assistance. This request was relayed to the Soviets who decided that the Czechoslovaks should support Cuba and thus "pave the way" for socialism in Cuba. There were two reasons behind this decision. First, because of the distrust between Castro and the Soviet Union, the Czechoslovaks were needed to provide a bridge and to convince Cuba to accept a Soviet presence in Cuba. Second, there was considerable concern that the United States would react aggressively if the Soviets were seen to move directly into Cuba. The use of Czechoslovakia was designed as a double deception, operating both against Fidel Castro and against the United States.

Raul Castro came to Czechoslovakia in the summer of 1960 to negotiate military assistance. As Secretary of the Defense Council, Sejna was responsible for his "care and feeding." When Raul arrived, he immediately was courted by Chinese diplomatic representatives, and more or less ignored by the Soviets, who were permitting the Czechoslovaks to handle the operation. Additionally, the Soviets avoided direct contact because they did not want the United States to conclude that the Soviet Union was behind the visit. Throughout the process of establishing a Soviet presence in Cuba, the Kremlin was very careful not to do anything that might trigger a U.S. response.

After several days, Sejna reported to the Soviet adviser, General Alexandr Kushchev, concerning the negotiations, and recommended that Khrushchev invite Raul Castro to Moscow. (A minor protocol problem was involved: the Soviet Ambassador to Czechoslovakia said the request had to come from Fidel Castro, and the Cuban leader was not about to ask.) Kushchev cabled Marshal Grechko in Moscow, who talked to Khrushchev over dinner that night. An invitation arrived the next day, but it was still several days before Fidel Castro agreed to allow his brother to visit Moscow. The visit lasted a week, during which time Raul spent three days with Khrushchev, who explained—as only Khrushchev could—what peaceful coexistence and the world revolution were all about. Khrushchev promised Raul Castro aid and support, but insisted that, initially, the Czechoslovaks should play the lead role to avoid alarming the Americans. The aspect of the operation that was designed to deceive Fidel was not discussed.

The main purpose of Raul's visit to Czechoslovakia was to obtain weapons. The Czechoslovak General Staff officers spent many days instructing Raul on military affairs and equipment, about which he was quite uninformed, and on designing Cuban defense plans and requirements. The Czechoslovaks agreed to provide half of the weapons to Cuba without charge and to sell the remainder on the basis of a Czechoslovak loan. In return, Havana agreed to have Czechoslovak military and political advisers stationed in Cuba and to send Cuban cadres to Czechoslovakia for training in military affairs, leadership, youth movements, party organization, and so forth. These advisers and this training signaled the real beginning of Soviet infiltration into the new Cuban government, since recruiting and inserting spies was an important covert task of the advisers and of the training process. This military assistance was thus the first major Soviet step toward taking over Cuba.

When Raul Castro returned to Prague from Moscow, he expressed considerable displeasure with the Soviet Marshals whom he had met and who had treated him like "a small boy." (At that time, Raul was 27 years old and most of the Soviet Marshals were in their seventies.) But he was genuinely excited about Khrushchev. As Raul exclaimed to Sejna, "No one ever explained things like Khrushchev!" After receiving Fidel's approval, Raul met with Czechoslovak military intelligence and agreed that Cuba would become a base of intelligence operations directed against Latin and North America. Cuba would be a revolutionary center in every sense of the word. He then reached agreement with the Minister of Interior (that is, internal security) on setting up a secret police apparatus in Cuba for counter-intelligence. Thus, Czechoslovakia was instrumental in building Cuban intelligence and counter-intelligence capabilities. This enabled Czechoslovakia to control the "reactionary" elements in Cuba, whether left or right, and to carry out a major deception against Fidel and the partisans by providing them with false information designed to turn them against the United States and toward socialism. This was the second major step for the Soviets in their plan to take control of Cuba. In the fall of 1960, the first supplies of Soviet bloc equipment, along with Czechoslovak military and intelligence advisers, were sent to Cuba to begin "paving the way for socialism."

The abortive Bay of Pigs in April 1961 was used by the Soviets to justify the building of a unified defense and the transition from a Czechoslovak to a Soviet presence in Cuba. This was the third major step toward securing full control. Operating through the Czechoslovak advisers, and with the assistance of "Cuban" intelligence, the Soviets convinced Castro that the United States was a serious threat, and that Soviet assistance was essential if Castro wanted to be the Lenin of Latin America. Finally, the Soviets urged Castro to dismiss his earlier "distrust" of the Soviet Union as the unfortunate result of a misguided Soviet ambassador to Cuba (who had led Moscow at first to believe that Castro, the son of a capitalist, could not become a true communist). In time, Castro accepted Marxism-Leninism and Soviet domination. On December 2, 1961, Fidel Castro publicly declared himself a Marxist-Leninist.

The Soviets convinced Castro that, in addition to a pervasive intelligence and counter-intelligence capability, he should build a strong military establishment, and Cuban defense plans should be coordinated with those of the Soviet Union. They warned that, if the United States attacked Cuba once, it would attack again and again. Furthermore, the Kremlin advised Castro that a small country like Czechoslovakia could not by itself provide the aid Castro needed. The Soviet Union would have to become involved directly.

In early 1962, Soviet advisers visited the Czechoslovak Defense Council to discuss Cuba. The time had come, they explained, for the Soviets to displace the Czechoslovaks in Cuba. The Soviets wasted no time. This exchange and Soviet assistance in the development of the Cuban military Operation Plan began immediately upon the arrival of the chief Soviet adviser, Colonel General Gusjev. General Gusjev was a tough administrator who had been responsible for crushing the bourgeoisie and establishing revolutionary power in the early 1950s in Czechoslovakia. The development of the Operation Plan was a signal event. In the communist system, this is the key plan that drives military readiness, mobilization, and equipment decisions as well as those of the "civilian" economy. As in other satellites, the Cuban Operation Plan was developed as part of the Soviet plan, with the same main contingency: general war with the United States. In developing the Operation Plan, the role of Soviet equipment, forces, and advisers was solidified. Advisers were placed in all key areas throughout the Cuban military, from regiment level to the very top: Raul Castro was the Minister of Defense and his adviser was General Gusjev.

In the spring of 1962, the exchange was accelerated. The rationale provided to Castro was that the introduction of sophisticated Soviet technology required Soviet technical assistance and direction. This was quite natural, since the Czechoslovaks simply were not able to install the new equipment. By the summer of 1962, the exchange had been completed and the Soviets were firmly in Cuba.

The final solidification of the Soviets in Cuba followed the missile crisis of October 1962. Fidel Castro was extremely displeased with the Soviet backdown. He went to Moscow, and for several days all members of the Politburo met with him to convince him that Khrushchev had made the correct decision; after all, the United States had promised not to intervene in Cuban affairs, and this would give the Soviets and Cubans time to initiate a long-term expansion of military capabilities in Cuba.

The final step in controlling Cuba was the buildup of the Party apparatus, which was developed as a reduced carbon copy of the Soviet system. To accommodate Castro's distrust of the former Party members who had shunned him because of his capitalist origins, a completely new Party was built out of the partisans. The Party was constructed with a Central Committee, as in the Soviet model, with its primary departments and control apparatus; a Defense Council where the main decisions were made; and the political apparatus in the departments and ministries, of which the ministries of Defense and Interior were the most important. By about 1966, the construction of the Party was completed and the Soviets were in firm control. By that time, the political commissars and Party control members had been educated and positioned, and 90 percent of the senior military officers were members of the Communist Party.

PERGAMON-BRASSEY'S
International Defense Publishers
in cooperation with the
Institute for Foreign Policy Analysis

List of Publications

Orders for the following titles should be addressed to: Pergamon-Brassey's, Maxwell House, Fairview Park, Elmsford, New York, 10523; or to Pergamon-Brassey's, Headington Hill Hall, Oxford, OX3 0BW, England.

Foreign Policy Reports

ETHICS, DETERRENCE, AND NATIONAL SECURITY. By James E. Dougherty, Midge Decter, Pierre Hassner, Laurence Martin, Michael Novak, and Vladimir Bukovsky. June 1985. xvi, 91pp. $9.95.

AMERICAN SEA POWER AND GLOBAL STRATEGY. By Robert J. Hanks. 1985. viii, 92pp. $9.95.

Special Reports

THIRD WORLD MARXIST-LENINIST REGIMES: STRENGTHS, VULNERABILITIES, AND U.S. POLICIES. By Uri Ra'anan, Francis Fukuyama, Mark Falcoff, Sam C. Sarkesian, and Richard H. Shultz, Jr. September 1985. xiii, 127pp. $9.95.

Special Reports: On the Agenda

(This "On the Agenda" series is published jointly with the International Security Studies Program of The Fletcher School of Law and Diplomacy, Tufts University.)

STRATEGIC MINERALS AND INTERNATIONAL SECURITY. Edited by Uri Ra'anan and Charles M. Perry. July 1985. viii, 90pp. $9.95.

Books

ATLANTIC COMMUNITY IN CRISIS: A REDEFINITION OF THE ATLANTIC RELATIONSHIP. Edited by Walter F. Hahn and Robert L. Pfaltzgraff, Jr. 1979. 386pp. $43.00.

REVISING U.S. MILITARY STRATEGY: TAILORING MEANS TO ENDS. By Jeffrey Record. 1984. 113pp. $16.95 ($9.95, paper).

INSTITUTE FOR FOREIGN POLICY ANALYSIS, INC.
List of Publications

Orders for the following titles in IFPA's series of Special Reports, Foreign Policy Reports, National Security Papers, Conference Reports, and Books should be addressed to the Circulation Manager, Institute for Foreign Policy Analysis, Central Plaza Building, Tenth Floor, 675 Massachusetts Avenue, Cambridge,

Massachusetts 02139-3396. (Telephone: 617-492-2116.) Please send a check or money order for the correct amount together with your order.

Foreign Policy Reports

DEFENSE TECHNOLOGY AND THE ATLANTIC ALLIANCE: COMPETITION OR COLLABORATION? By Frank T. J. Bray and Michael Moodie. April 1977. 42pp. $5.00.

IRAN'S QUEST FOR SECURITY: U.S. ARMS TRANSFERS AND THE NUCLEAR OPTION. By Alvin J. Cottrell and James E. Dougherty. May 1977. 59pp. $5.00.

ETHIOPIA, THE HORN OF AFRICA, AND U.S. POLICY. By John H. Spencer. September 1977. 69pp. $5.00. (Out of print.)

BEYOND THE ARAB-ISRAELI SETTLEMENT: NEW DIRECTIONS FOR U.S. POLICY IN THE MIDDLE EAST. By R. K. Ramazani. September 1977. 69pp. $5.00.

SPAIN, THE MONARCHY AND THE ATLANTIC COMMUNITY. By David C. Jordan. June 1979. 55pp. $5.00.

U.S. STRATEGY AT THE CROSSROADS: TWO VIEWS. By Robert J. Hanks and Jeffrey Record. July 1982. viii, 69pp. $7.50.

THE U.S. MILITARY PRESENCE IN THE MIDDLE EAST: PROBLEMS AND PROSPECTS. By Robert J. Hanks. December 1982. vii, 77pp. $7.50.

SOUTHERN AFRICA AND WESTERN SECURITY. By Robert J. Hanks. August 1983. vii, 71pp. $7.50.

THE WEST GERMAN PEACE MOVEMENT AND THE NATIONAL QUESTION. By Kim R. Holmes. March 1984. x, 73pp. $7.50.

THE HISTORY AND IMPACT OF MARXIST-LENINIST ORGANIZATIONAL THEORY. By John P. Roche. April 1984. x, 70pp. $7.50.

Special Reports

THE CRUISE MISSILE: BARGAINING CHIP OR DEFENSE BARGAIN? By Robert L. Pfaltzgraff, Jr., and Jacquelyn K. Davis. January 1977. x, 53pp. $3.00.

EUROCOMMUNISM AND THE ATLANTIC ALLIANCE. By James E. Dougherty and Diane K. Pfaltzgraff. January 1977. xiv, 66pp. $3.00.

THE NEUTRON BOMB: POLITICAL, TECHNICAL AND MILITARY ISSUES. By S.T. Cohen. November 1978. xii, 95pp. $6.50.

SALT II AND U.S.-SOVIET STRATEGIC FORCES. By Jacquelyn K. Davis, Patrick J. Friel and Robert L. Pfaltzgraff, Jr. June 1979. xii, 51pp. $5.00.

THE EMERGING STRATEGIC ENVIRONMENT: IMPLICATIONS FOR BALLISTIC MISSILE DEFENSE. By Leon Gouré, William G. Hyland and Colin S. Gray. December 1979. xi, 75pp. $6.50.

THE SOVIET UNION AND BALLISTIC MISSILE DEFENSE. By Jacquelyn K. Davis, Uri Ra'anan, Robert L. Pfaltzgraff, Jr., Michael J. Deane and John M. Collins. March 1980. xi, 71pp. $6.50. (Out of print.)

ENERGY ISSUES AND ALLIANCE RELATIONSHIPS: THE UNITED STATES, WESTERN EUROPE AND JAPAN. By Robert L. Pfaltzgraff, Jr. April 1980. xii, 71pp. $6.50.

U.S. Strategic-Nuclear Policy and Ballistic Missile Defense: The 1980s and Beyond. By William Schneider, Jr., Donald G. Brennan, William A. Davis, Jr., and Hans Rühle. April 1980. xii, 61pp. $6.50.

The Unnoticed Challenge: Soviet Maritime Strategy and the Global Choke Points. By Robert J. Hanks. August 1980. xi, 66pp. $6.50.

Force Reductions in Europe: Starting Over. By Jeffrey Record. October 1980. xi, 91pp. $6.50.

SALT II and American Security. By Gordon J. Humphrey, William R. Van Cleave, Jeffrey Record, William H. Kincade, and Richard Perle. October 1980. xvi, 65pp.

The Future of U.S. Land-Based Strategic Forces. By Jake Garn, J. I. Coffey, Lord Chalfont, and Ellery B. Block. December 1980. xvi, 80pp.

The Cape Route: Imperiled Western Lifeline. By Robert J. Hanks. February 1981. xi, 80pp. $6.50 (Hardcover, $10.00).

The Rapid Deployment Force and U.S. Military Intervention in the Persian Gulf. By Jeffrey Record. February 1981; revised edition, May 1983. viii, 83pp. $7.50 (Hardcover, $12.00).

Power Projection and the Long-Range Combat Aircraft: Missions, Capabilities and Alternative Designs. By Jacquelyn K. Davis and Robert L. Pfaltzgraff, Jr. June 1981. ix, 37pp. $6.50.

The Pacific Far East: Endangered American Strategic Position. By Robert J. Hanks. October 1981. vii, 75pp. $7.50.

NATO's Theater Nuclear Force Modernization Program: The Real Issues. By Jeffrey Record. November 1981. viii, 102pp. $7.50.

The Chemistry of Defeat: Asymmetries in U.S. and Soviet Chemical Warfare Postures. By Amoretta M. Hoeber. December 1981. xiii, 91pp. $6.50.

The Horn of Africa: A Map of Political-Strategic Conflict. By James E. Dougherty. April 1982. xv, 74pp. $7.50.

The West, Japan and Cape Route Imports: The Oil and Non-Fuel Mineral Trades. By Charles Perry. June 1982. xiv, 88pp. $7.50.

The Greens of West Germany: Origins, Strategies, and Transatlantic Implications. By Robert L. Pfaltzgraff, Jr., Kim R. Holmes, Clay Clemens, and Werner Kaltefleiter. August 1983. xi, 105pp. $7.50.

The Atlantic Alliance and U.S. Global Strategy. By Jacquelyn K. Davis and Robert L. Pfaltzgraff, Jr. September 1983. x, 44pp. $7.50.

World Energy Supply and International Security. By Herman Franssen, John P. Hardt, Jacquelyn K. Davis, Robert J. Hanks, Charles Perry, Robert L. Pfaltzgraff, Jr., and Jeffrey Record. October 1983. xiv, 93pp. $7.50.

Poisoning Arms Control: The Soviet Union and Chemical/Biological Weapons. By Mark C. Storella. June 1984. xi, 99pp. $7.50.

National Security Papers

CBW: The Poor Man's Atomic Bomb. By Neil C. Livingstone and Joseph D. Douglass, Jr., with a Foreword by Senator John Tower. February 1984. x, 33pp. $5.00.

Books

Soviet Military Strategy in Europe. By Joseph D. Douglass, Jr. Pergamon Press, 1980. 252pp. (Out of print).

The Warsaw Pact: Arms, Doctrine, and Strategy. By William J. Lewis. New York: McGraw-Hill Publishing Co., 1982. 471pp. $29.95.

The Bishops and Nuclear Weapons: The Catholic Pastoral Letter on War and Peace. By James E. Dougherty. Archon Books, 1984. 255pp. $22.50.

Conference Reports

NATO and its Future: A German-American Roundtable. Summary of a Dialogue. 1978. 22pp. $1.00.

Second German-American Roundtable on NATO: The Theater-Nuclear Balance. A Conference Report. 1978. 32pp. $1.00.

The Soviet Union and Ballistic Missile Defense. A Conference Report. 1978. 26pp. $1.00.

U.S. Strategic-Nuclear Policy and Ballistic Missile Defense: The 1980s and Beyond. A Conference Report. 1979. 30pp. $1.00.

SALT II and American Security. A Conference Report. 1979. 39pp.

The Future of U.S. Land-Based Strategic Forces. A Conference Report. 1979. 32pp.

The Future of Nuclear Power. A Conference Report. 1980. 48pp. $1.00.

Third German-American Roundtable on NATO: Mutual and Balanced Force Reductions in Europe. A Conference Report. 1980. 27pp. $1.00.

Fourth German-American Roundtable on NATO: NATO Modernization and European Security. A Conference Report. 1981. 15pp. $1.00.

Second Anglo-American Symposium on Deterrence and European Security. A Conference Report. 1981. 25pp. $1.00.

The U.S. Defense Mobilization Infrastructure: Problems and Priorities. A Conference Report (The Tenth Annual Conference, sponsored by the International Security Studies Program, The Fletcher School of Law and Diplomacy, Tufts University). 1981. 25pp. $1.00.

U.S. Strategic Doctrine for the 1980s. A Conference Report. 1982. 14pp.

French-American Symposium on Strategy, Deterrence and European Security. A Conference Report. 1982. 14pp. $1.00.

Fifth German-American Roundtable on NATO: The Changing Context of the European Security Debate. Summary of a Transatlantic Dialogue. A Conference Report. 1982. 22pp. $1.00.

Energy Security and the Future of Nuclear Power. A Conference Report. 1982. 39pp. $2.50.

International Security Dimensions of Space. A Conference Report (The Eleventh Annual Conference, sponsored by the International Security Studies Program, The Fletcher School of Law and Diplomacy, Tufts University). 1982. 24pp. $2.50.

Portugal, Spain and Transatlantic Relations. Summary of a Transatlantic Dialogue. A Conference Report. 1983. 18pp. $2.50.

Japanese-American Symposium on Reducing Strategic Minerals Vulnerabilities: Current Plans, Priorities and Possibilities for Cooperation. A Conference Report. 1983. 31pp. $2.50.

National Security Policy: The Decision-Making Process. A Conference Report (The Twelfth Annual Conference, sponsored by the International Security Studies Program, The Fletcher School of Law and Diplomacy, Tufts University). 1983. 28pp. $2.50.

The Security of the Atlantic, Iberian and North African Regions. Summary of a Transatlantic Dialogue. A Conference Report. 1983. 25pp. $2.50.

The West European Antinuclear Protest Movement: Implications for Western Security. Summary of a Transatlantic Dialogue. A Conference Report. 1984. 21pp. $2.50.

The U.S.-Japanese Security Relationship in Transition. Summary of a Transpacific Dialogue. A Conference Report. 1984. 23pp. $2.50.

Sixth German-American Roundtable on NATO: NATO and European Security— Beyond INF. Summary of a Transatlantic Dialogue. A Conference Report. 1984. 31pp. $2.50.

Security Commitments and Capabilities: Elements of an American Global Strategy. A Conference Report (The Thirteenth Annual Conference, sponsored by the International Security Studies Program, The Fletcher School of Law and Diplomacy, Tufts University). 1984. 21pp. $2.50.

Third Japanese-American-German Conference on the Future of Nuclear Energy. A Conference Report. 1984. 40pp. $2.50.

Seventh German-American Roundtable on NATO: Political Constraints, Emerging Technologies, and Alliance Strategy. Summary of a Transatlantic Dialogue. A Conference Report. 1985. 36pp. $2.50.

Terrorism and Other "Low-Intensity" Operations: International Linkages. A Conference Report (The Fourteenth Annual Conference, sponsored by the International Security Studies Program, The Fletcher School of Law and Diplomacy, Tufts University). 1985. 21pp. $2.50.